- audio book
- written form
- E Book
- paperbook

Book card

Pardeshi, Kalyani (co-author), 2019, *Rise: In Pursuit of Empowerment,* Reach for Greatness Publishing

UNBULLIED!

14 TECHNIQUES TO SILENCE THE CRITICS EXTERNALLY AND INTERNALLY

KALYANI PARDESHI

Copyright

Title: Unbullied! 14 techniques to silence the critics externally and internally

First published in 2019

ISBN: 978-107916-0369

Book design: Colette Mason of www.letstellyourstory.com

Editing: Chloe Smith of www.chloeivyrose.co.uk

This book is not endorsed by or affiliated with Brooks Gibbs, Dandapani or any other website or organization mentioned in this book in any way.

DEDICATION

This book is dedicated to every victim of bullying. May you find hope, direction, and healing through these words. May you find strength, courage, and conviction to help you move past the hurt, pain and anguish you have felt because of your experiences. It is my sincere desire to give you hope through this book, to show you that you are perfect just the way you are, to enable you to believe in yourself just as I believe in you. May your healing begin from the very first chapter of this book.

CONTENTS

ACKNOWLEDGEMENTS

The first person I wish to credit is Colette Mason of www.letstellyourstory.com without whom this book would have remained just a crazy dream. Her coaching and guidance were pivotal in getting this book out of my head and onto my laptop in less time than I had ever imagined were possible. The accountability and guidance she offered was nothing short of phenomenal. I was sitting with this book idea for five months and in a mere month, her tools helped me get it to where it is today. She also designed the cover of this book knowing exactly what I wanted. Thank you, Colette.

Faith Rodriguez of www.faithrodriguez.net for being my intuitive mentor, for always encouraging me every time I doubted this path I had taken, which was more often than I would like to admit. Her guidance, mentoring and encouragement became a crutch I leaned on a lot. This book would never have materialised without her support.

A huge shout out to Avinash Kumar who is not only an amazing and extremely reliable friend of mine, but he is the wonderful designer of the incredible images in this book. He had to work with a very tight deadline and the quality of the images speak for themselves. He brought the images to life by giving so much character and personality to them. If you are considering hiring a designer, get in touch with him already!

(You can reach him at mahamedhavi.com/workwithme) or email avinashvlog@gmail.com).

Gopal Krishnan of www.visualmarketer.com for christening this book with its title. Arun Bhardwaj of Arun's images (www.facebook.com/arbwaj) for the author photo.

Chloe Smith of www.chloeivyrose.co.uk who not just edited this book but became my "go-to" person every time I felt unsure of what I was doing. Mentioning her here as just the editor of this book would be a huge misstatement. She took on this project with immense passion and was always available to answer any questions I had, patiently and thoroughly. Her professionalism is truly astounding!

Another name totally worth mentioning is Olivia Angelescu (www.oliviaangelescu.com) who is nothing short of an angel. She came to my rescue, literally, when I was struggling to market this book.

A massive thank you to all my beta readers (and their parents) who read the first draft of this book and provided eye-opening nuggets! Their valuable feedback went a long way in making this book what it is today. Thanks Raphaela, Emma, Ailbhe, Avery, Dagmar, Derrick, Jarl, Christiaan, Arun, Nabiyah, Tyren and Shyla.

I would also like to acknowledge my wonderful husband and children who gave me the courage to share such intimate details of what I had faced. I am so grateful for their love and comfort as I painfully re-lived some of the most traumatic experiences of my life. Their love soothed the pain and helped me heal.

I have a long list of numerous friends who stood by me while I worked on this project, constantly reminding me of the importance of what I was doing, cheering me on every time I felt like quitting. I want to thank them for being present, often virtually, when things became overwhelming. Their unwavering support will always remain close to my heart. The list is too long and all I can say is that I am deeply grateful to every single one of you. You know who you are.

INTRODUCTION

This book is the ultimate collection of every technique I have used, personally, to combat bullying and the emotional scars thereof, successfully!

ABOUT ME

I was born in Lusaka, Zambia, and moved to South Africa when I was ten years old. When I moved, it was the peak of apartheid years, and my parents told me to keep a low profile because I didn't have the right skin colour for anything I had to say to matter.

I've faced bullying throughout my life: in school, in the workplace, and within family. I think it's safe to say that this has given me enough experience to talk about this subject with the benefit of hindsight.

Where am I today? Geographically speaking, I live in Canada with my family. But, jokes aside, I'm in a place where I don't tolerate any form of bullying, even if it means standing alone. I would rather walk alone in the right direction than with a crowd in the wrong direction. I no longer fear bullies and isolation because I don't feel crushed about being left out by a crowd who doesn't accept me as I am.

My intention with this book is to show you how to get to where I am today, and how to do it now, not thirty years later.

WHY I WROTE THIS BOOK

Early in 2018, I attended an anti-bullying workshop at the school my kids attend. The idea of the workshop was to teach the kids how bullying affects the victims. It was supposed to be a deterrent to bullying. While it was all great on the day itself, it didn't take too long for the bullies to be back at it again. My daughter even asked me – "what was the point of that workshop if kids are still bullying?"

It bothered me that the workshop wasn't enough to make a difference. What more could we do? What could we do differently? I've had years of experience dealing with bullies, so I decided to write it all down, including my personal experiences of bullying when I was in school. But I also decided to include action that you, as the victim of bullying, can take today. More often than not, we feel helpless against bullies and the intention of sharing these actions is to empower you, the reader of this book, to help you see that you do have control and you are not helpless at all.

I have read many stories about celebrities who were bullied when they were younger and yet went on to succeed in life. My thought was this - how about a story of a Plain Jane who turned out just fine and much stronger despite being bullied in her life?

Truth be told, this is the first time I'm recounting the bullying I faced for the sole purpose of making a difference in this world.

Sharing my story, experiencing the pain as I write this has had me in tears many times but because I feel that in order to help others, I need to re-live my pain and share what I went through, I am pushing past the pain.

WHO THIS BOOK IS FOR?

Though I have been bullied throughout my life, I chose to focus on the bullying I faced as a teenager because it was a time where I hadn't yet learned how to be resilient and strong. This book is a list what I could have done at the time, but with the knowledge, experience and strength I have today. I share these experiences and lessons with you, teenagers and young adults, so that you don't have to wait years to develop the skills and resilience I have today, which took me many, many years to build. Teenagers and young adults are at an impressionable age, horrible experiences tend to leave scars, and some scars last a lifetime.

Bullying affects how we respond to situations. It makes us change who we are at our core, so we don't cause ripples, so we don't draw attention to ourselves. It is my sincere hope that my book will help those battling difficult circumstances find light and direction in the darkness, to believe in who they are and stay true to who they are, rather change themselves based on what others say about them. It is said that it takes a village to raise a child. Well, circumstances have changed, as has the village, but I believe that with the right tools, the village and children can succeed and soar.

WHAT THIS BOOK COVERS

Whilst I'm sharing my own bullying experiences, it's not to sadden you but to show that I really do understand what it feels like to be a victim of bullying. I am one of you.

In every chapter, I've shared exercises detailing every technique that I have used personally which you can use to overcome any bullying you may be facing while also discovering how strong you really are, and you may surprise yourself. If you do these exercises and follow the techniques diligently, I have no doubt you will be in a far better place than you are right now.

I also have a section that answers your burning questions on bullying. I posted about this on social media and gathered all the questions I had received and attempted to answer them to the best of my abilities.

Just as with anything, it's only as good as the effort you put towards it. You might look at the exercises and say, "this is too much work, I don't want to do it." Sadly, having this approach will be of little help to you. Remember, if you are looking for a helping hand, look at the end of your sleeve.

HOW TO USE THIS BOOK

You will need sodium chloride, a beaker, a Bunsen burner as we write and cast nasty spells on our bullies.

Just kidding, it's not rocket science. All you need is a journal ready and maybe some loose paper. Read each story — some of them might feel familiar to you, others perhaps not. Either way, I recommend doing the exercises and familiarising yourself with each technique even for the stories unfamiliar to you. Preparation is key, irrespective of what you might be facing. Repeat the exercises as many times as you need to, so you feel confident about the direction you are taking and in turn, you feel confident within yourself.

These exercises help you create a guide of sorts within you, your benchmarks so I am trying to get you in touch with your feelings so you can use your feelings as a compass to show you the way out of every sticky situation, a way in which you feel happy within yourself and with your surroundings.

The purpose of writing things down is to help yourself remove the emotion from the problems you're experiencing. It moves the things you've experienced from your subconscious mind to your conscious mind because you're reliving it. It enables you to process your thoughts and emotions in a more rational way, essentially removing yourself from the situation – therefore allowing you to process it and move forward.

Now that you know more about me, why I wrote this book and how to get the most out of it, let's gets started. But remember, don't half-ass the work and expect glorious results. Autumn Calabrese, a celebrity fitness trainer whom I respect immensely, rightly says, "it's not about how badly you want something, it is about how hard are you willing to work for it."

So, my question to you as you dive into this book is – how hard are you willing to work to change your circumstances for the better?

KEEP IN TOUCH

I would love to know how this book helped you (or not – there is always room for improvement for me as well)! Go ahead and drop me a message while you do so, feel free to check out some of the articles and posts I have on my page! I can't wait to hear from you!

If you are interested in having me as a guest speaker at your event or if you would like to reach out to me to present a workshop, here is where you can contact me:

- www.facebook.com/kalyanispeaks
- www.facebook.com/kalyanipardeshi

ONE: IT WAS A WHISPER, AT FIRST

> *Have you ever been called names? You know how it makes you feel, right? It affects your self-confidence and makes you feel like you're not good enough.*

IT WAS A WHISPER, AT FIRST

When I was two months shy of my twelfth birthday, my parents sent me away to what was considered a prestigious boarding school in another country. It was prestigious because it admitted students on a non-racial basis, which was significant considering the apartheid era we were then living in. If I remember correctly, it took around eight hours to drive there including stopping at the border.

There weren't any good schools where my parents lived and being Asian (specifically, Indian), education is the one thing that is given utmost priority. Living in apartheid South Africa, access to good schools was limited especially because I didn't have the "right" skin colour.

To be honest, I was excited to go away. It made me feel so grown up and the new wardrobe I got added to my joy as it would for any girl that age. My brother had already been at the school for a year and he seemed to have settled in quite well, but he didn't share much whenever I asked him about the school.

I was too young to see that as a warning sign.

I remember the day my father left after dropping me off. He'd stayed in a hotel for three days while all the new students went through orientation. I wanted to look mature and not like the daddy's girl that I was, so when he was leaving, I gave him a quick peck on the cheek and ran off to be with my new friends.

I regretted that for as long as I could remember, on days when I felt so alone and so scared, I berated myself for not giving my father a hug, for not holding onto him. It was as if doing so would have somehow helped me hold onto hope and give me strength when I was tormented by my bullies.

HOW I GOT THESE NAMES

Growing up, my parents were somewhat conservative. I am glad to say that this has changed drastically over the years. When buying my new wardrobe for boarding school, they bought quite a few long dresses for me. Though I had been a tomboy growing up, I was attempting a different style in my adolescent years. I loved the dresses, all lovely pinks and blues. I felt like a princess.

But there was a catch. These dresses were really long, maybe even oversized. The idea was to cover my legs as much as possible – remember when I mentioned my parents were somewhat conservative? This is what I meant.

Within a few weeks at boarding school, I started hearing whispers as I walked past.

"Sis Mary. Sis Georgina."

At first, I thought it was my imagination but after a while, I knew these were names I was being called. I just didn't know why. Every hiss, every "Sis Mary", every "Sis Georgina", drove thorns into my heart. Why? What had I done? What did these names even mean? It didn't help that I was missing my parents and my home terribly. There was not a day that went by when I didn't cry, and the name calling aggravated every bit of hurt and loneliness I felt.

I somehow managed to make it through three months, the first term, crying a lot and just feeling miserable. We got around a month off and it was good to go home, but, as the saying goes, all good things come to an end. After spending four glorious weeks at home with my parents enjoying an environment familiar to me, in my safe haven, eating home cooked meals, I had to go back to boarding school for the second term.

The name calling continued.

Preparing for a new term at the school, I was unpacking my suitcase after which I started making my bed, putting on the sheets with great care, smoothing out any wrinkles while breathing in the scent of "home" i.e. the fabric softener that my mom used, my only source of comfort. Three girls were walking outside, past an open window as I made my bed. "Sis Mary," one girl chimed, and the other two girls laughed. I buried my head into my unmade bed, planting my face deep in my sheets as I cried and cried, seeking comfort from the scent of home but finding none.

I finally plucked up the courage to ask a friend of mine what these names meant. She told me the names implied I wore the same thing as a nun. Upon seeing the hurt on my face, she tried to ease the blow by saying that it was because I was innocent and naive. The damage had already been done, but I was grateful that she was honest with me.

What did I do about the name calling? I did what anyone would do - I complained to the teachers. If you've ever done this before then you'll know exactly how I felt when I did this. You know you feel bad enough about the names to want to do something, to want to act but there is also a hesitation - what if I'm blowing things out of proportion? I will answer this question in a bit. The teachers downplayed my feelings and the actions of my bullies.

"Oh, it's just a name, it doesn't mean that's who you are."

"Sticks and stones may break your bones, but words don't hurt you, right?"

"Kids are just being kids, they are silly. Don't take it so seriously."

"Kids call each other names all the time, they are just playing around with you. Take it as a game."

These were just some of the responses I got from my teachers.

By not validating how I felt, my teachers made me feel like a wimp. Apparently, name calling was normal and a part of building camaraderie, while my reluctance to accept this made me an outcast. I felt isolated and terribly lonely. Their response to my complaints made me doubt myself. The lack of action taken against my bullies for name calling made me question myself - was I really a wimp? Was all of this really normal? And was I some sort of a loser who wasn't strong enough, brave enough, or cool enough to tolerate and overcome it?

Not only did I doubt myself, but I doubted the very values I was raised with - be kind to others, as much as you can be. Why didn't my bullies have these values? Were they even important? It was like my very foundation was crumbling. Everything I believed in and was brought up to trust was smoke and mirrors, it only applied to me while everyone else was allowed to break the rules.

Answering the question I asked earlier - what if you're blowing things out of proportion?

In short, **you're not.**

If no one else says this to you, I will. You are not blowing this out of proportion.

Here's the problem: as we ease into becoming teenagers and adults, we are subtly taught to censor our feelings because that's the supposed definition of maturity. In censoring our feelings, we drown out our intuition. Our intuition is our compass which guides on what is "right" and what is "wrong". However, when we let logic take over, that is when we feel caged and helpless.

The best example of this concept is the way teachers approached name calling. They saw it as "team building", almost like you're being initiated to be part of a group, a clique, in fact. Yes, a part of me wanted to ask my teachers how they would feel if the students called them names like "loser teacher", "pumpkin face" or "Frankenstein", but I didn't have the courage to.

Most kids put up with this behaviour towards them because speaking out wasn't worth the drama it would create. But in keeping the peace, they were in pieces inside.

Do I regret speaking to the teachers about the name calling? No, even now I would rather take action than suffer in silence. I had the comfort of knowing that I tried. As I reflect on these experiences as an adult, I now realise that I didn't have the words to explain the depth of my anguish.

If you're wondering what lessons I learnt from this, here they are.

I am not what my bullies call me, I am whom I choose to be. Keep persisting until you get the result you want, keep telling those in charge what is happening, insist on action being taken against your bullies. Don't quit until you get the results you want.

EXERCISE: APPLYING THE "SOMERSAULT" TECNIQUE

I love to call this the "somersault" technique – turning name calling on its head! Grab a paper and a pen or pencil. This technique is something I learnt as an adult, and it requires reprogramming your thinking. As you do this exercise, remember, you are not what your bullies call you. Opinions don't pay bills, if they did, we all would be millionaires.

Back to the paper. Draw a huge T from the top of the page all the way to the bottom - cover the entire page. On the left-hand side of the T, at the top, write the title "Names my bullies call me" and on the right-hand side of the T, at the top, write the title "Who I really am". As the titles say, on the left-hand side, list out all the names you are called by your bully, so on mine, I would have "Sis Mary" and "Sis Georgina" on the left-hand side.

On the right hand side, write down the exact opposite word of the names you are called. But there is a catch, the positive names you choose for yourself have to be believable for you. So, in my case, the names I was called referred to my attire as a nun's habit. We all know what the opposite of a nun is, yeah, I don't want to say it out aloud. In such a case, what I would choose to do is focus on my personality and what I see as good traits within myself. If you find yourself in the position I was in with the name calling, then use the exercise from chapter nine in conjunction with this one. More on this in chapter nine. For this exercise, here are some examples you can use:

```
Nerd = Intelligent

Loser = Winner

Idiot = witty/smart

Fat = Perfect for my height

Skinny = perfect for my height
```

You get the idea.

Every positive word or set of words you write about yourself has to be something you believe about yourself, otherwise it won't work. If you're struggling with this list, I suggest you ask an adult you trust how they see you and go with what they say.

Once your list is complete, take a pair of scissors and cut the page down the middle so you have two separate pieces of paper - one with positive words and one with the names your bullies call you.

Take the piece with the negative words and do one of these three things: burn it (with an adult's supervision), tear it up into tiny pieces and recycle it, or flush it down the toilet.

This simple act is an emotional release, doing so will make you feel better. So, what's your next step?

Take the positive words and write them out on some nice stationery. Make a few copies, and if you have a phone, take a picture of it and use this image as your screensaver. Place the copies in different locations as visual reminders of who you really are. Stick one on the mirror, read it out aloud as you get ready in the mornings. Put one in your pencil case and deliberately look at it every time you reach for a pen or pencil.

After ten days, change the locations of these visual reminders. This will trigger your mind to notice them as if for the first time. Stick one on your laptop, one on your hairbrush, one on your lunch kit. You get the idea.

The purpose of this exercise is removing negative thoughts about yourself based on what others say to you and to reprogram your brain to think only the best about yourself. Remember, what others say about you doesn't become your reality unless you let it. You have all the power, let's acknowledge this together. If you are wondering what to say to stop the name calling, that comes up in a separate chapter, for now, I want to focus on helping you build a positive image of yourself.

I want you to focus on building your self-belief before you give a befitting reply.

SUMMARY

Remember:

- You are not what your bullies call you, you are who you choose to be. Who are you going to choose to be? What are you going to allow to define you? Your bullies' words? Absolutely not!
- Though your bullies' words may break you down, you can take your power back. Repeat the "somersault" technique as often as you need to. The more you do it, the better you will feel about yourself.
- Those who are insecure in themselves feel the need to put other people down, to bring them down to their level. Always keep in mind that no one can make themselves look better by putting others down.
- You can't expect others to believe in you if you don't. Belief in yourself starts with you. Start here, start now - you are a winner!
- Speak to yourself in loving, nurturing and compassionate words, how you treat yourself through this trauma is how others will treat you. Your healing starts with you, within you.

"It is your responsibility to show the world how to treat you by the way in which you treat yourself."

~ Lisa Nichols ~

TWO: THE CLICK OF A TONGUE

Bullying can become physical, and more often than not, perpetrators aren't dealt with in an effective way. It is important to note that physical or sexual bullying is a criminal offence and should be reported to the police, not just school authorities.

THE CLICK OF A TONGUE

When I went away to boarding school, it was the early years of swearing. TV shows and movies had barely introduced curse words. I understand that this is somewhat very common these days but back in the day, it wasn't. Naturally, there was a crowd of people in the school who thought it was cool to throw around a few "S" and "F" words. I still have no idea how this makes someone look cool.

Like any other school, physical education was part of our curriculum. We would get to play different kinds of sports ranging from volleyball, to swimming, to netball, to soccer.

HOW IT ALL WENT DOWN

On this particular day, we were playing netball. Because a lot of the kids had gotten into the habit of swearing, the teacher set a strict rule: if anyone swore, it would be called a foul and the ball would go to the other team.

Both teams were playing hard, eager to win as if there was a gold Olympic medal at stake. It was just a game, yet everyone was so serious, so competitive and so eager to win.

My team was down by a few points and I approached a girl on the opposing team. She was a lot larger in size than I was. She had the ball and I was going get the ball from her or block her at least, so I thought. As she was trying to get past me, something triggered her, and she muttered "sh*t!". I was the unfortunate individual who heard this.

I didn't know how to censor myself in those days – and I still struggle with this at times – so I blurted out, rather loudly, "she swore", pointing at her. The PE teacher came over and handed the ball to me. That girl shot me a dirty look, one that had me covered in goosebumps. I brushed it aside and continued to play. My team went on to win and I was really happy about it.

Incidentally, the girl who swore also happened to be the same girl who gave me the names "Sis Georgina" and "Sis Mary". I will refer to her as TWB henceforth – The Worst Bully.

At the end of the school day, we usually went back to our dorm rooms to clean up and get ready for dinner time. When I was waiting to go for dinner, I noticed TWB approaching me out of the corner of my eye. My palms became clammy and my hands started to tremble, but I mustered up the courage to look her in the eye when she stood opposite to me.

"I did not swear!" TWB yelled. I wasn't sure what she wanted me to do. Rewind the entire incident and make it better for her or apologise?

I wasn't about to apologise when I know what she said, I heard it with my own ears and so did my team members, but no one spoke up for me.

A crowd of girls had gathered around us. I felt like I was put on the spot, with more than a dozen set of eyes staring at me, waiting in anticipation, to see what I would say or do next. TWB was a known bully and I had stepped on a bear's paw.

"You did swear, that is why the teacher gave my team the ball. Stop denying it." I blurted out before I lost the courage to do so. Then she clicked her tongue at me. In any other country, this would be inconsequential but in this particular country, it is considered to be an insult – a really bad insult.

Without even thinking about it, I clicked my tongue right back at her. If she could do it, why not me? The next thing I felt was a sharp sting on my left cheek.

It took me a few seconds to realise that TWB had slapped me, really hard. Tears stung in my eyes, burning as I fought to keep them from spilling over. Tears of humiliation, shame, embarrassment and fear. Then, she clicked her tongue at me again, as if to challenge me.

Though I knew I couldn't fight her back as she was twice my size and had the support of the other girls watching this drama unfold, I refused to be insulted by her. How dare she? If it was okay for her to do it to me then I would do it back to her. Without thinking of the consequences, I clicked my tongue back at her - if I couldn't fight her, the least I would do is not allow her to insult me. Bad decision.

Crack!

It sounded like my jaw dislocated as she planted yet another thunderous slap across my left cheek. This time, I couldn't hold the tears back. They came spilling over, streaming down my cheeks, one of which was now swollen and likely to bruise.

There were more than a dozen girls, sitting on the beds surrounding this scene. No one got involved, no one stood up for me. They chose to sit on the sidelines sneaking in a giggle or two at my plight.

TWB seemed satisfied with her deed, muttered something inaudible to me and walked away. The crowd dispersed, leaving me alone to cry. I crumbled to the floor and hugged myself in a futile attempt to console myself. I sobbed like a baby in distress, but no one came forward to comfort me.

What did I do about it? When I managed to compose myself, I went to the teacher on duty in the boarding house that day. With my reddened and swollen cheek as evidence, I had no doubt that serious action would be taken against TWB. These were the days before cell phone technology, so the swollen cheek was the only proof I had of the physical bullying. As for witnesses, I wasn't surprised that no one was willing to support me when I went to speak to the teacher.

I poured my heart out to her, telling her exactly what had happened between sobs, sniffs and gasps for air, sometimes choking on my own tears, my swollen cheek burning from the tears. All she offered me was a tissue or two. No comfort and barely any validation.

"Kids will be kids, Kalyani," she said.

"If one more teacher tells me 'kids will be kids', I will holler and scream my lungs out," a voice bellowed in my head.

These very words were stuck in my throat, forming a lump which I desperately tried to swallow so I could speak coherently. So that I could try to explain exactly how deeply I was hurt. Not just physically but emotionally too - the humiliation I felt being watched by so many girls, being put on the spot with all attention on me, the disgrace I felt at the laughter of the girls and TWB as she shamed me for telling the truth. How could this teacher possibly even begin to understand how I felt?

"Oh well, I am sorry this happened, I will speak to her and get her to apologise to you," the teacher continued, interrupting my thoughts. She then went on to dismiss me and I walked back to my dorm room, slowly, every step laboured as if my feet were encased in cement. My shoulders hung as I felt defeated. Even the teachers wouldn't stand up for me. "Sorry". A single word that was supposed to take away the pain.

The pain of humiliation, shame, disgrace and physical pain. How? I didn't think it could.

As the teacher said, she spoke to TWB, who then went on to apologise to me. Suddenly, I was expected to be nice and friendly with her and vice versa. If you ask me honestly, that stinks. What would I have preferred at the time? A more severe punishment such as suspension. The way it was handled made me feel that TWB never grasped the concept that there are serious consequences to her actions. So much for making an example out of her.

What lessons did I learn? That is all in the exercise with this chapter – what I should have done. Hindsight is 20/20 after all.

EXERCISE: APPLYING THE "LOCKED AND LOADED" TECHNIQUE

I have always believed that preparation is half the battle and that prevention is the best cure, hence I present to you the "locked and loaded" technique.

If you ever feel that you could possibly be physically assaulted by your bully, always ensure that you aren't alone. Make plans ahead of time, talk to friends, teachers, whoever you need to so as to ensure you are never alone with this bully.

What if you find yourself alone with this bully as I did? In my case, I never expected her to assault me because I hadn't seen her do this to anyone else. Avoid confrontation, there is no need to defend yourself, trust me, your bully isn't interested in what you have to say in your own defence. They just want to show you who's boss. Looking back, when she confronted me, I should have walked away rather than trying to defend myself.

If ever you are physically assaulted, at the first physical contact, run and holler as loud as you can, ensuring you get as much attention as possible. Get yourself to a safe place, find adults - parents or teachers - and stay with them. In the day and age of cell phone technology, someone is bound to be recording a video of this, so you'll have evidence of what happened. Some schools have CCTV cameras, ensure to take advantage of that too if ever you find yourself in this situation.

It is so important to know that physical and sexual bullying or assault is a criminal offence and needs to be reported to the police, not just to the school authorities. Make sure you let the right people know what happened so that they can take corrective action accordingly and don't give up until you get the results you want.

Physical or sexual assault isn't something that should be taken lightly.

SUMMARY

- Be aware of bullies around you, take note of anyone you feel physically threatened by.
- Observe to identify simple physical altercations such as pushing someone around.
- Keep the notes from the exercise handy so any time you find yourself in a situation similar to mine, you will know exactly what to do to be heard and for appropriate action to be taken against your bully.

"Strong people stand up for themselves, but the strongest people stand up for others."

~ Chris Gardner. ~

THREE: "SURE!" THE SILENCING WORD

> *The one thing I always wanted to be able to do was to shut my bullies up. But who'd ever thought it could be so easy?*

"SURE!" THE SILENCING WORD

Our music teacher assigned my class a mini project where we had to speak about our favourite musician and share a little bit of their music with the class. Sounds easy enough, right? Not for me. Let me explain.

I grew up in a home where the one thing we listened to the most was the radio and, on the radio, the only thing we listened to was the news. Sounds boring, right? But it was who I was at the time and I learnt to embrace and accept myself that way. I knew almost everything that was happening in the world. This helped me a lot with General Knowledge tests.

For everyone else, this project was a doozy. But I had no idea what to do. Of course, I knew of famous artists of that time - Michael Jackson, Madonna, Bon Jovi etc. I had even heard their music which was often played in the school's dormitories. But I didn't really have a favourite, never mind know enough to talk about them.

I do have a confession to make. I could've winged it if I tried but I was afraid to for the very simple reason that if I didn't know enough, it would give my bullies another chance to make fun of me. I couldn't risk it.

My safest bet was to do my project on someone the students hadn't heard of, so there wouldn't be any opportunity to make fun of me - or so I thought. Whether they were interested in this person and his music was the least of my concerns, I was just trying to protect myself.

I spoke to a friend of mine about this and she understood how I felt. Her parents listened to classical music and she suggested I do my project on Frédéric François Chopin, a Polish composer and pianist who wrote music for solo piano. She said she would borrow the cassette from her parents for the part of my project where I needed to play the music.

I compiled my project by researching him in encyclopaedias, and my friend brought the cassette from home for me to play in the music class as she had promised to.

The structure of the project was simple; we had to speak about the musician, their music, and their life, and then play a full song by them.

I got up in front of the class and spoke about Chopin while everyone listened and snickered. The teacher seemed impressed because I didn't choose a popular artist as everyone else did.

And then it was time to play the music. But I'd made a big mistake; I'd never listened to the music before. So, I put on the cassette and I played the music, intending to play a full song as instructed.

There was beautiful piano music that swelled through the room, and then it paused, so everyone assumed it was over and started clapping. So, then I also assumed it was over. As I was getting ready to press stop on the cassette player, the music continued, and everyone laughed at me.

I stopped the player and I walked away thinking. "Okay, you know what? It's done. I got through it. It's done and I'll get a mark for it rather than failing music."

So, what did my bully do? Incidentally, she wasn't even in the same class as I was. She heard about my project from classmates of mine who obviously found this very funny. She approached me after school. I was sitting on the grass on the side of a small hill minding my own business, just being by myself enjoying the sun and I saw her approaching me. I pretended not to notice. However, my hands became clammy, my knees felt weak, just as well I was sitting down. I became nervous as my mind went into overdrive - I didn't know what to expect. She was one of the popular girls at school and another known bully.

She opened her mouth and said, "Hey, we're having a social tonight." A social was a bit like a party, but in the confines of a boarding school.

She went on to say, "I wanted to borrow your music from your music project for it."

My mind was racing inside. I knew she was using this as an opportunity to make fun of me, laugh at me and belittle me –

that was the theme of the bullying I faced. And though it seemed like forever, I did respond.

All I really wanted to say to her was, "you know that this is not music you can dance to, it is classical music." I really wanted to say that. But something clicked inside of me. And I stopped. Instead, I said,

"Sure, absolutely. You can borrow it. Just let me know what time you need me to get it to you."

She was so stumped by my answer. This was the first time I'd ever seen her totally dumbstruck.

She said, "Okay. Yeah sure," and got up and walked away.

She missed out on an opportunity to belittle me because I did not give her the reaction that she wanted. And that is a lesson

I learnt in this process: more often than not, bullies are teasing and picking on you because they want that reaction out of you.

Another example I want to mention here occurred much later in my life as an adult. I have a family member who is a bully. He's said some horrible things to me to elicit a reaction.

He barked at me, "I don't care about you. I don't want to see your face." While I responded with, "That's awesome. Thanks for letting me know." He was shocked because he's used to people grovelling when he says things like that and usually responding with statements like, "Oh, please don't say that. I'm sorry." I didn't and for the first time since I have known him, he was at a loss for words. This was an amazing and immensely empowering feeling for me.

LESSONS I LEARNT

This was a very interesting experience for me because it taught me that bullies usually call names and pick on you because they want a reaction. It makes them feel powerful, like they're in control.

The lesson I learnt is that the minute I react in anger and I get defensive, I've let my bully win. It doesn't mean that what they say about you is true; it just means that you're not allowing what they say about you to affect you. The minute you start fighting and getting defensive you lose the battle because they get a laugh out of it. They see that they're in control and you're no longer in control, and that's the situation you want to avoid.

Ultimately, the lesson that I learnt was that I was not going to let what other people think about me and say about me affect me.

I was also giving power to my bullies by reacting, by freaking out and by getting defensive.

The most important lesson to learn in all of this is to know that what others say about does not become your reality unless you let it. You give power to their words by reacting to it. And in giving a nonchalant, unexpected response, you disempower them.

It's not about getting back at them. It's not about trying to put them down the way they put you down because that way you're no different from them. If it hurts you to be called the names that they call you, to be told the things that you are told, why would you do that to somebody else? Honestly, revenge is not the answer.

EXERCISE: APPLYING THE "SURE PUMPKIN" TECHNIQUE

I love to call this technique, the "sure pumpkin" – giving your bullies a totally unexpected response which silences them. On a blank piece of paper, draw a giant T.

On the left-hand side of the vertical line, write out what your bullies say to you, every single thing you can remember. On the right-hand side of the vertical line, write down nonchalant responses, ensure none of your responses are in any way a defence of yourself or an attack on your bully.

Once you've made your list of nonchalant responses, *memorise* them. One of the biggest issues that I always had when dealing with my bullies was not being quick witted. I didn't have the answers to shut them up. It was on the odd occasion that I had the right answers, and then giving those right answers and watching the bullies shut up, where I realised, "Oh, wow, that's what I need to do. Just give them a response they are not expecting." It was my "aha" moment.

When somebody comes up to you and says what they say to you, you can give these prepared neutral responses. You have a whole arsenal of neutral responses that you have memorised. You don't even have to be quick witted. You have the answers. You can give them the answers and walk away with your dignity, respect and pride intact.

SUMMARY

- Bullies say what they do to elicit a reaction from you which gives them a sense of power and control. If you don't react in the way they expect you to, and you disempower them with your response, you win.
- You don't have to have the last word, but you can always have the right words to leave your bully speechless.
- Ensure to have enough of these responses, memorise them so you are never at a loss for words.

*"Other peoples' perception of you ain't none of your business.
Everything is a set up for your next best season"*

~ Lisa Nichols. ~

FOUR: DON'T CRY...

Sometimes we choose not to share how we really feel in fear of being judged or even ridiculed. But how would you feel if someone told you to bottle up your feelings? What if sharing your emotions was no longer your choice, and you were forced to stifle them?

DON'T CRY

I had been at boarding school for a month or so, and I was still terribly homesick. There wasn't a day that would go by when I didn't cry, but I was not the sort of person who would go into the washroom and cry. I cried very openly.

I missed my parents as well as the safety and security of being in my home. I missed home cooked food. I missed the comfort of home. Basically, I missed the comfort of having my parents around and the security of being around things that were familiar to me. It was really hard.

As is typically known, boarding school food sucked. You know there's only so much you can take on your own without parental support. Think of sleepovers at a friend's place - you'll stay one night, maybe two nights. Soon after a couple of nights, you would want to go back home, no matter how difficult things might be there. There's security associated with being in an environment that's familiar to you that you've known since childhood.

From the moment you're born, the moment you open your eyes this is what you have always known as home and associate it as your safe haven. I made it no big secret that I was homesick. I cried a lot, while everyone else seemed to have adjusted well. In fact, I don't remember anyone crying the way I did, unless if they cried in the privacy of the washroom or at night, when everyone was asleep.

There were a few friends who comforted me. There was one in particular who I remember was much more patient than everyone else. She was always there whenever I cried. She'd stop doing what she was and give me a hug and hold me until all the tears ran out.

A couple of weeks into boarding school, I remember sitting down and somebody handing me a letter. I didn't know what to make of it, thinking it was just an ordinary letter. I had no idea what was written in it.

I gingerly opened it up, my hands trembling as I unfolded the piece paper, careful not to tear it. I didn't have the patience to read every word, so I briefly scanned what was written after which I burst into tears. I was heartbroken. This letter had been signed by almost every single girl in the two dormitories, including the girl who used to comfort me. I felt betrayed by her.

What was in this letter? Why did it hurt me so deeply?

In this letter, I was told to stop crying. I was told to stop being a wimp, to grow up and accept that I was away from home. Everyone else was doing just fine.

How did I see it? I was being told that there was something wrong with me due to which I couldn't adjust. Why did I have to cry in front of everybody?

Part of the reason which I now understand, as an adult, is that my crying publicly made it harder for everyone else because they were fighting their own feelings about being away from home. While I was very vocal about mine, the others tried very hard to block their feelings.

Back then, as a child, I was never taught to bottle my feelings. I wore my heart on my sleeve, and that's something I still do to this day.

But it was so hard for me to digest the fact that there were people around me that I didn't know so well who decided to judge me and my personality.

I did not like being singled out, put in the spotlight and being told that my emotions weren't valid, that what I was feeling wasn't allowed. As if I needed permission from others on what and how to feel. Somehow, I felt what my parents taught me about being open regarding my feelings wasn't true and I shouldn't share how I felt. Basically, I was told what to do with my feelings and I didn't like that, it made me feel very uncomfortable, like I was being controlled by others.

I never really censored myself and I thought that being told what to do by people I barely knew was terribly unfair. I have never felt so lonely as I did that day, especially because there wasn't a single person who validated how I felt and said to me, "You know what? It's okay for you to feel that way. It's natural. How can I help?"

Kindness like that did not exist.

LESSONS I LEARNT

I think one of the most important lessons I learnt through this letter from my dorm mates was that I couldn't be *that* open about my feelings. I had to pick and choose with whom I could be open. While I know it is a pretty obvious lesson in this day and age, it was different for me back then.

It's a whole new ball game when you're living with a group of teenagers for three months at a time.

It's a different setup when you go to school every day. You come home to your parents, where even if you cannot explain how you feel, you can express it in your frustration and your parents understand and listen because they know how hard it is to be a teenager. They allow you the space to be frustrated. Sometimes they get frustrated, but it is your safe environment where you can share your feelings even if those are feelings of explosion because you are so angry, because nobody understands how you feel better than you do.

It is very difficult to censor your feelings for such an extended amount of time especially because there really isn't anyone you can talk to. It trained me to censor my feelings and share only when and where necessary, and only with the people that I felt comfortable in sharing my feelings with.

This experience taught me to actively seek out people who would understand how I felt, validate my feelings without judging me or making fun of me. Yes, people like this do exist but it requires some work to find them. They were my "keep it real" friends.

EXERCISE: APPLYING THE "BTY" TECHNIQUE

What is the "BTY" technique? It is "being true to yourself", allowing yourself the space to feel what you need to without judgement. Journal how you are feeling. Write a letter to yourself or to a parent or to somebody whom you trust, a "keep it real friend". Writing things down provides clarity and helps you get your thoughts organised so that your message is clear and concise. If it so happens that you can't speak to your parents, seek out an uncle or an aunt or a cousin, somebody whom you can open up to. Write to them and share how you feel, no matter what emotions you may be experiencing.

This exercise does two things. First, it will help you get agony out of your heart and out of your mind transferring it onto paper. It's a transfer of energy. There are a lot of gurus who talk about this, writing your feelings down transfers all that negative energy, the negative feelings within yourself onto paper so it is no longer a part of you. Doing so will make you feel emotionally lighter.

The other thing it does, is it releases emotions because it validates how you feel. You are giving yourself the validation you seek. More often than not, rather than expecting an outsider to say to you, "it's okay to feel that way", emotional growth starts with you telling yourself that it is okay to feel the way you do. Nobody has the right to tell you that you cannot feel a certain way. They're not inside your body. They're not inside your heart, they're not inside your mind. They don't know how you feel, only you know how you feel.

So, write that down. If you are comfortable in doing so, share it with somebody that you care about, someone who matters to you and vice versa. This will give you the extra external validation that you need. I will give you a sample of this letter. If you're struggling with words, I will provide a series of words that you can pick from and it will help you write down what you're feeling. Share it with somebody who understands how you feel.

This will kickstart your healing process.

LETTER SAMPLE

(to someone you trust, sharing how you feel)

Hi _____

Let me start by saying that I am so grateful to you for always giving me the space to share how I feel while also accepting how I feel. I am writing this letter because I am in a difficult situation, one that makes me feel *hopeless, frustrated, anxious, depressed, angry, sad, disheartened, dejected, demoralised* (choose words that describe how you feel from here or choose your own words).

I feel this way because _____ (describe what it is you are facing because of your bully, what is it that your bully does to you - no matter how small or insignificant it may seem, give every possible detail, tell it as it is).

I am reaching out to you in hopes that you can help me with this, in hopes that you can take action which I am unable to, to put an end to this situation which is making me so miserable. Please know that it has taken a lot for me to share this with you but now that I have, all my hope lies with you in helping me.

Thank you,

(Sign off this letter in the way that describes you best whether it is "Love ____" or anything else that makes you, you).

LETTER SAMPLE

(letter to yourself, validating how you feel)

Hi _____ (insert your name here),

I am writing this letter to you to let you know that you are right. You are right to feel the way you do, no one can or should tell you that your feelings don't matter. They cannot decide how you should feel, only you know how you should feel. Don't allow anyone that power over to you to decide for you what you should feel.

I am here validating you and how you feel. You are right and it is absolutely okay if no one else agrees with how you feel, you don't need anyone to believe in you, belief in you starts with yourself. So please don't be discouraged if no one else agrees with you, remember to live life on your terms, never allow anyone to discredit your feelings and never allow anyone to make you doubt yourself.

You've got this!

Your cheerleader forever

(Sign your own name here).

Read this letter to yourself as often as you need to, as a pep talk to keep encouraging yourself especially when you don't have anyone else doing it for you. Your feelings are valid, I am here to tell you that.

SUMMARY

- Sharing your feelings should be a choice that you get to make and shouldn't be forced on you. But you can definitely smarten up about whom you choose to share these feelings with and how much to share.

- Bottling up how you feel shouldn't be an option, healing starts with opening up about how you feel. The more you share how you feel, with the right people, the easier it becomes for you to deal with your emotions in a healthy way.

- Often, we don't share how we feel in fear of being judged or in fear of being made fun of. Sometimes, it is a case of trying to fit in. I am sure many were homesick like I was, but they weren't as vocal about it as I was due to these very fears. As I said above, share how you feel with the right people who will understand, love and support you through the dark times.

- If you feel there is no one you can trust with your feelings, then opt to speak to a school counsellor or call a local kids helpline – they will keep your confidence and you will get to ease some of the pain you are experiencing in a safe setting.

"Tears are God's gift to us. Our holy water. They heal us as they flow."

~ Rita Schiano. ~

FIVE: SAY HER NAME!

We have all experienced peer pressure at one time or another. When we're so eager to be accepted into a clique, we do things our gut tells us not to. What do you do when you're in this situation?

SAY HER NAME!

It was a night like any other - or so I thought. I woke up to giggling and laughing. I was tempted to turn the other way and just go back to sleep, but curiosity got the better of me. So, I climbed out of bed to see what was going on.

As I walked through my dormitory, the common shower area, and tip-toed towards the larger dormitory, the noise got louder and louder.

There was a pillow fight going on, and it looked like tons of fun. But then again, I hadn't been invited to take part. I was the odd one out, so I chose to turn away and go back to sleep. I didn't want to participate in the shenanigans. I had a feeling that it wasn't going to end well.

I climbed back into bed, and I tried really hard to fall asleep. I even put my head under the pillow, attempting to block out the noise if possible, but failing miserably.

It must have been about half an hour later when I heard the first sounds of trouble. Everything was silent except for one voice that was thundering rather loudly. Again, curiosity got the better of me. So, I climbed out of bed, and I slowly snuck into the larger dormitory where the pillow fight was going on. Ensuring I wasn't spotted, I peeked out of a corner to see what was really going on.

All the girls were standing around and watching the drama unfold in front of them. The bully I spoke of a few chapters ago, the one who tried to make fun of my choice in music for my music project, was at the centre of the commotion. Let's call her MB (My Bully) for the purpose of this story.

MB was forced to sit atop a chest of drawers. There was another girl who was hitting her really hard with whatever she could find. Whether it was a rolled-up magazine or slapping her with her bare hands, this girl was just smacking MB while the latter sat there with her head hung, her hair pulled forward covering her face, probably hiding the tears as they streamed down. MB did not fight back.

One of the things that this bully, who was beating MB up, did, was ask every girl standing around watching this commotion call out her name. After which, she would repeat that girl's name making MB promise that she wouldn't be afraid of the said girl. Once MB confirmed what the bully said, she was slapped hard - as if it was supposed to be some sort of stamp of approval. Signed, sealed and delivered. With at least twenty girls standing there, you can guess how many times MB was slapped.

While I stood there, watching in shock, I realised I had the perfect opportunity to have my bully beaten up.

But here's the thing. I didn't do it. I was the only girl in that room who did not call out her name.

Now I know you're probably wondering what's wrong with me. It was a perfect opportunity to get back at my bully for trying to make fun of me and my choice for my music project. Despite it being the perfect opportunity, why didn't I take it?

There were a number of reasons for it. The first one was that I felt it was unfair. She just tried to make fun of me and getting her beaten up for this was not fair punishment in my eyes. I also thought that two wrongs don't make a right. Another reason was that it just didn't feel right to me. I know what it feels like to be on the receiving end of any form of bullying behaviour and I would not subject someone else to it. That's why I wouldn't do it and I didn't do it.

I found out much later on why this bully was beating MB up. It was because MB had hit the bully's friend really hard with a pillow so much so that she knocked the wind out of this girl. The bully kind of lost it with MB and beat her up quite badly.

So that is why I did not participate in something where someone else was getting hurt because I know what it feels like to be hurt. I would be just like my bullies.

LESSONS I LEARNT

The obvious lesson I learnt is that two wrongs don't make a right. Yes, I had the perfect opportunity to get back at my bully. But how would I have felt about it afterward? I don't think I would've felt good, because I would've just stooped down to my bullies' level. I didn't want to be a bully. I never wanted to be a bully. So, knowing how that felt I was not going to subject another human being to it.

The other most important lesson I believe I learnt through this process was trusting my feelings. The thing is, as we grow older, we tend to follow logic more than we do our feelings or our intuition. Our feelings are our compass, it shows us right from wrong. We often ignore some of those inner feelings because we want to fit in with those around us. And that's when we accept behaviour that isn't respectful towards us, because we don't want to stand out saying, "Well, everyone else accepts this, but I won't."

The key lies in trusting your instincts. If something doesn't feel right to you then you shouldn't be doing it, no matter how unpopular it may make you. Even if you have to walk the path alone, do what feels right to you. If you end up doing what's popular and what's acceptable, you're going to feel miserable inside yourself because you're not doing what feels right to you.

EXERCISE: APPLYING THE "FIT" TECHNIQUE

Nope, I am not going to ask you to break out into a cardio routine nor will I ask you to lift some weights. What is the "FIT" technique? It is all about trusting your own feelings and instincts. For this exercise, I would like you to journal.

Was there ever a time in your life where you did something just to keep the peace or not to be singled out? You did something but deep inside yourself, you knew it wasn't the right thing to do. How did it make you feel? Did it gain you the popularity you were seeking? Did it bring you the peace you sought? At what cost?

I've done this many times. One of the best examples I can give you is being a people pleaser. It was just easier for me to be a people pleaser instead of rocking the boat by saying, "You know what, this is not who I am." This is something that took me years to learn. It's made me very unpopular, but I'm okay with it. I would rather be unpopular than do something that makes me unhappy.

So, when you journal about these incidents, make a list of the friends who might have made you do this. Are they still your friends? Remember to write down how you felt about what you did.

Obviously somewhere along the line, you weren't comfortable doing what you did, but you did it anyway. So, write three things down:

- How did it make you feel?
- Why did you do it?
- What could you have done instead?

Don't worry about the consequences of what would have happened if you had done what you wanted to do instead. The idea behind this exercise is to help you recognise that you do have a choice, in every situation. Now, I'm not talking about avoiding chores your parents give to you, that you have to do. That's part of growing up.

For example, if someone is being picked on and everyone's picking on them, it doesn't mean you have to join in, even if it means you lose your friends. Anything that makes you feel uncomfortable is an indication that you're not supposed to be doing it. Sometimes part of growth is discomfort, but that discomfort is more like a nervous discomfort because you know it's going to help you, so you have to do it. But any discomfort that gives you an icky feeling inside, that's what you avoid doing. So, journal away and keep this as your little guide to point you in the right direction whenever you're not sure what to do.

SUMMARY

- Sometimes it is far more painful to fit in than it is not to. I'm sure you have heard many people say that two wrongs don't make a right and that is exactly why I didn't succumb to the peer pressure.

- Ask yourself if fitting in is costing you inner peace and if the answer is "yes", then it's time to change.

- You shouldn't have to do anything that makes you uncomfortable just to be accepted by your peers.

- Remember acceptance starts with you, if you cannot accept yourself as you are, why would others?

- Doing the "right" thing will help you build self-confidence. The more you do it, the better it is for your confidence. This, in turn, becomes an attractive quality that will draw more of the right kind of friends to you.

- In closing, remember what C.S. Lewis said, "Integrity is doing the right thing when no one is watching." In trying to keep the peace, in trying to fit in, don't start a war within yourself.

"You would have no peer pressure if you cared less about the opinions of others."

~ Jeff Moore. ~

SIX: YOU STINK

> *It's bad enough being bullied by girls, but the boys didn't leave me alone either. They found their own way to ridicule me, which made them snicker and laugh while making me wish the earth would swallow me whole.*

YOU STINK

Teenage years are very confusing. Your body is going through changes while you also experience emotional turmoil. Hair is growing in unimaginable and unspeakable places, freaking you out. It is like being on a roller coaster without a safety harness. But you don't need me to share all of this with you as you learn this in health class. However, the one thing I do want to talk about is body odour - yes, sweat. You had it before, but it didn't have the smell to it and now it does.

It's hard enough dealing with all these changes, even having a parent close by to support you through it. It was even harder for me being away from my mom in this difficult phase. I did not have her close by to hold my hand, figuratively, through these changes. To be brutally honest, I don't even remember her talking to me much about it beforehand. Things were different back then. It wasn't like we had access to books on this subject, perhaps books weren't even written about the subject. It was just something that was rarely spoken about. In those, health class would only be taught in grade ten whereas now health class starts in grade four and continues through grade five and six.

Like every other teenager, I was going through all these changes, and I was trying my best to keep up. There was a group of boys who found it really funny to cover their noses and laugh every time I walked past them. As I walked past, they would turn around, snicker, look directly at me and say out loud, "You stink. You give off a bad smell." After uttering these words, they would burst out in fits of laughter as they noticed the hurt look on my face.

This made me very self-conscious. I know I was doing the best I could to stay hygienically clean. But the fact that they said this to me bothered me a lot.

In addition, I guess my mind was so naive that I didn't think that if, in fact, I really did stink, I am sure everyone else would have said something to me, but it was just this group of two to three boys who would corner me or leap out of a corner and say to me, "You stink, you give off a bad smell."

They made me feel very uncomfortable. It was hard enough dealing with these changes without my mom around and to top it off, having people making ugly comments left me miserable.

I remember how I reacted. I would shower for longer and I would scrub myself with soap so hard that my skin would be red from all the scouring I did. I used so much soap that I pretty much went through a bar of soap within a week. After the torture of a painful shower, I would fumigate myself with deodorant.

The fumigation was to ensure I didn't stink, but no matter what I did, they always picked on me. They always cornered me or surprised me by jumping out of a corner and blurting out, "You stink."

This eventually escalated into insulting matches where they would learn insults in my native language and taunt me. It hurt really bad. What could I really do about it? I couldn't go to the teachers and say, "Oh, these boys say that I stink." It sounds pretty lame, doesn't it? What would the teachers do about something like that? They would probably say, "Just ignore them. Boys will be boys." Or would they go to them and say, "Don't say she stinks. It is not a nice thing to say"?

What can one really do in a situation like this? Is there a solution? I don't know. All I know is that I changed myself. I changed the way I took care of myself because I wanted to put an end to the nastiness.

Did it put an end to the nastiness? No. It didn't. What did I get out of changing my routine? Three months of sore skin from scrubbing myself. That's all I got out of it. And obviously, I did not stink. I guess they got some sort of a kick out of my reaction to their words.

I don't understand why they got a kick out of it. I'm not the sort of person who goes around hurting other people just for my own personal pleasure. That's not who I am. So, I ended up changing myself, changing my routine, changing the way I took care of myself because I wanted to put an end to the nasty words. It was a lose-lose situation for me because I didn't put an end to the nastiness, and I was actually hurting myself by scrubbing so hard because I didn't want to be told I stank.

LESSONS I LEARNT

The most important lesson I learnt through this experience was the fact that I shouldn't change myself, nor should I change the way I do things on the basis of what others say about me. Doing so will not put an end to their brutal words. It reminded me that what others say about me is none of my business. Someone saying something about me doesn't make what they say, true.

I should choose to change myself only if I want to become a better person.

No matter what you do, no matter how much you change yourself, you will not be able to please everyone. It doesn't work that way. They will still find something to torment you with. But remember, it's not because there's something wrong with you. It's because there's something wrong with them. Normal people don't go around breaking other people down.

You see, when I was called the names Sis Mary and Sis Georgina, I couldn't change. I wasn't interested in changing the way I dressed. I just accepted who I was, even though it hurt.

But that lesson versus this lesson taught me that even if I did change, it wouldn't put an end to the torment and there is nothing wrong with me, but everything wrong with my bully.

So, the most important lesson in this particular incident for me and for you, my reader, is that don't change just because people say things about you. Self-reflect to see if what people are saying is coming from a nasty person or if it is coming from someone who genuinely cares about you.

And finally, change because you feel it's the right thing to do. Trust your instincts.

EXERCISE: APPLYING THE "DA" TECHNIQUE.

Don't worry, you don't have to go to law school to use this technique! I love to call this the Devil's Advocate technique, you'll see why. In this exercise, you should journal times in your life where you have changed because of something someone said to you.

In each instance, try to identify:

- Was it because you felt that changing yourself would put an end to the bullying or the nasty comments?
- Or did you change yourself because you wanted to become a better person? Was this change part of your personal growth?

And then for each instance, ask yourself, how did this said change make you feel?

So, where you changed because you wanted to put an end to the nastiness - how did this change in yourself make you feel about yourself? Did it make you feel good? Or did it make you feel icky inside?

Where you were changing for personal growth, for where you felt that you're becoming a better person by making this change, how did this change make you feel afterward?

Use your feelings as a benchmark and a guide.

SUMMARY

- The point of sharing this story compared to being name called was to show you that sometimes, without our own realisation, we allow what bullies say to us to change or affect our behaviour.
- We change what we do and in turn, who we are in futile attempts to silence our bullies. In doing so, we show our bullies that they have won because we succumbed to their words.
- With the name calling, I didn't change who I was, I didn't change my attire because I couldn't. However, I did change my habits because of what the boys said. I let them win. Don't fall for the same mistakes as I did.
- Before you change who you are, ask yourself this: am I changing because I want to, because it is to my benefit, or am I changing because I want my bullies to shut up?
- When you change because you want to, because it benefits you and is part of your personal growth, you will be happy through the process.

"Absorb what is useful, discard what is not, add what is uniquely your own."

~ Bruce Lee. ~

SEVEN: AN UNLIKELY SAFE HAVEN

Do you have a place you consider a safe haven? A place where you feel protected and even comforted? Surprisingly I found an unlikely safe haven in the hell that was boarding school.

AN UNLIKELY SAFE HAVEN

In boarding school, every single student had a privilege which used to rotate every two weeks. What was this privilege? To be the first or second person to use the showers every morning, after which everyone else would get their turn, following a clockwise pattern of the bunk beds in the dorm room.

The downside of having this privilege was being assigned chores. These chores were either bathroom duty or laundry duty. Bathroom duty included drying the wet floors of the shower area with a squeegee and draining out the area outside of the showers. The showers were communal - open showers with only walls separating the stalls and no shower curtain, so you can imagine the amount of water that spilled out.

The other one, laundry duty, meant lugging a heavy laundry basket up a hill to the laundry room twice a week. These laundry baskets were huge cylindrical bins with handles on the sides. They were so heavy that it took two people to carry them up the hill.

At the end of the school day when the laundry was washed, dried and folded, those on laundry duty were supposed to meet at the laundry room and carry this gigantic laundry basket back down to the boarding house. All the laundry was labelled with name tags, so you just needed to sort it out and put it on each student's bed.

On the mornings of laundry duty, I remember having a partner who would help me carry the basket uphill. At the end of the day, I was usually the first person to show up to collect the laundry. My partner would always be late because she was in a different class and I suspect she wanted to bunk laundry duty, knowing I would do it anyway.

Under the pretext of waiting for my partner, I used to hang out in the laundry room, almost as if to hide from the world outside. When I say hideout, I didn't hide behind anything, I just sort of stayed there. I observed all the ladies working hard, emptying out the washing machines, loading the clothes into the dryer, emptying out another drier and folding the clothes.

They always had a smile on their faces and laughed as they worked. They got to know me by first name within no time at all. I remember just staying there longer than I needed to, taking in that warm, humid, musky smell, especially in the winter.

I used to overstay my welcome was because I felt safe. I felt that as long as I was there amongst these adults, no one could hurt me or pick on me. Despite waiting much longer than needed, my partner wouldn't show up. This was a blessing in disguise for me as I would stay there for as long as I possibly could. When my presence became a little too obvious, I would carry the basket down the hill back to the dormitory by myself.

Hanging out in the laundry room wasn't just about feeling safe. It was about acceptance. This was the place where being myself was enough. This place was my safe haven. I felt accepted by these women who didn't judge me for the clothes I wore or for how I may have smelled or even for my appearance. They were just happy to have me there and chat with me. I used to talk to them about almost anything while they would share their stories about their homes and their lives.

That dark, dingy, musty, perhaps even mouldy and rat-infested place became my unlikely safe haven.

The biggest deal for me was that these women made me feel "normal" and didn't isolate me in any way. I was holding on to that environment, that space and those people because they welcomed me with open arms. I was one of them and by sharing their stories with me, they made me feel included. I finally felt like I was good enough to be a part of a group. It just felt good to be with these women and I didn't get to feel good very often.

LESSONS I LEARNT

The most important lesson I learnt in this was that even if there's a huge crowd of people picking on you and not accepting you as you are, there will always be someone who will accept you as you are and will not judge you. They will consider you as one of their own.

Another lesson I also learnt is that there is always a safe haven no matter how difficult the situation may seem. The problem is, we tend to focus so much on the hurt we feel from those who are bullying us that we forget we do have safe spaces.

We need to be able to identify these safe havens and utilise them as much as we can to reach that place, emotionally, where we feel strong, comfortable, loved and accepted.

Recognize the safe havens and make sure that you use them as much as you need to. The more confidence and love you feel in it, the stronger you will feel when you have to face your bully because you recognize that it's not you who is at fault. For argument's sake, if everything was wrong about you, then there wouldn't be a single person on this earth who would accept you and love you just the way you are. I don't have a shred of doubt that you have a network of family and friends who love you dearly. Try to focus on your safe havens. There are plenty of them, just look for them consciously seek them out and identify them.

EXERCISE: APPLYING THE "SAFETY NET" TECHNIQUE

We all have a safety net which we don't always notice. In this exercise, I want you to identify your safe havens. They don't have to be a place, it can be a person or a group of people. It could be a good teacher, a group of friends, your parents, or close friends of your parents.

While I understand that your parents and close friends of your parents cannot be with you when you're in school, the idea is to identify the safe haven so that whenever and however you can, you can spend time with them. That's what is going to help you heal - being around people who build you up rather than people who break you down.

Write them a letter explaining your situation, explaining why you might need to spend a little more time with them because it helps you. Put them in a "trusted person" position. Believe me, when someone is put in that "trusted person" position they will do everything in their power to help you, more so when they recognise that you're battling a difficult time with a bully. They will take the initiative to be there for you and they will help build you up. Your environment is what helps you form your strength. So, while you can't change your bully, you can definitely control your environment by choosing people who lift you up and encourage you.

Identify your safe havens. Write letters to these people.

SAMPLE LETTER

Hi _____ *(insert name of the person you are writing to)*

I thought to reach out to you for a little help. Perhaps you might not know this but I am battling through a difficult time because of a bully/bullies *(exclude this sentence if the person you are writing to already knows this and put this sentence instead:* As you already know, I am battling through a difficult time because of the bully/bullies I spoke to you about*)*.

I am writing this letter to you to let you know that you are one of those few people who help me cope through this struggle. You give me hope and courage, you remind me that there is nothing wrong with me simply by accepting me the way I am and including me in everything you do *(omit this last part if this letter is to a parent/teacher as they will always include you in everything by default)*.

You are a "trusted person" for me. While I understand that you cannot be with me at all times, I do want you to know that it helps me a lot when you are *(omit this sentence if this letter is to a teacher or a parent and use this sentence for a friend:* when we hang out, I find my bullies tend to stay away – thank you for creating this "safety net" for me*)*.

I really appreciate that you are there for me.

(Sign off this letter in a way that best describes you).

Those who read this letter will automatically feel encouraged to be there for you more and help you through this. In helping others, we feel good about ourselves and, fact is, we all want to feel good about ourselves. While clothes and accessories may provide happiness and excitement, it's only temporary, true happiness comes from helping others with no ulterior motive.

SUMMARY

- Every so often, we forget that we have a safe haven, and sometimes, we need to create that safe haven for ourselves.
- The need to cope through tough times can kick start our minds into searching and even creating those safe places and environments as I did.
- These safe havens give us some respite from the agony we face daily. The more respite we get, the stronger we become to face difficulties coming our way.
- Seek out your safe havens as often as you need to, utilise them as much as you need to. The more you do, the better it is for you.

"Every child should have a safe place in their life."

~ Joe Manchin. ~

EIGHT: A TRIUMPHANT LOSER

> *I had a personal victory but was then made fun for it. Any feeling of triumph I experienced was doused by teasing. Why did this happen? Why did I still feel like a loser? What did this bitter experience teach me?*

A TRIUMPHANT LOSER

Our school year was divided into three terms. We went to school from January until the end of March, then we had April off and then we went back to school from May through to July. We went back to school from September through to the end of November and we would have December off.

After a year and a half of being an easy target and being bullied, I'd had enough. I was halfway through grade nine when I returned from my April vacations back to boarding school.

As I watched other kids being bullied, I realised nothing had changed, and nothing would ever change. I was surrounded by bullies. Even though, at the time, they hadn't actively started bullying me, I figured it was only a matter of time before I became the source of their entertainment. I was done, completely done. There was no way on Earth that I was willing to put myself through any more torture for the sake of getting an education.

There was no way I could force myself to be there and to continue studying there. When I was watching all this injustice towards innocent people unfold around me, I felt completely powerless to stop it. I was counting down the days before I was targeted again.

Everyone except me seemed happy to be there. Perhaps it was just me, perhaps something was wrong with me. I wasn't happy to be away from my family. It was really hard, and I had nothing left in me to try to stick it out for just one more term.

I remember making that phone call to my dad, my voice trembling as I said to him, "I can't do this anymore. I understand that it has barely been a few days since I came back here but I just can't do this anymore."

At the time. I didn't understand the concept of energy. Have you ever felt a bad vibe in some places? You know how a place gives you an uncomfortable feeling? This is what boarding school was like. I recognised that vibe being in that environment so although I wasn't actively being bullied at that time, just feeling the vibe from other kids who were being bullied set my emotions off. Though they seemed to be handling it well, all I could think of was when was it going to be my turn. It gave me a bad feeling which led me to believe that I just couldn't do this anymore.

I said to my Dad, "Please take me home. I don't want to be here, I just can't be here."

As I mentioned earlier, it was an eight-hour drive one way from my parents' home to this boarding school. My dad did the trip barely two or three days before, yet I was asking him to do it again, for my sake.

I felt proud that I'd finally taken a stand and even though it might have been perceived as running away from the situation, I just decided that there was no way I could fix it. So, I chose to walk away, which I think is more acceptable now. Back then bullying was considered as character building.

I truly believed that there was a better way to help me build my character, to improve my personality traits than being picked. Truly, it was destroying me.

My dad was confused. He didn't know what to do. However, at the end of that conversation, he asked me if I was sure about my decision as I was walking away from the opportunity to get an exceptional education. I told him that I would rather walk away from a good education with my emotions, self-esteem and my sanity intact, than be broken down to such an extent that I couldn't cope.

I heard myself apologise to him, over and over, "I am sorry, I can't do this anymore. I am not as strong as you thought I was." Sadly, that is how I saw it. I saw it as not been strong enough to cope with mental torture and physical abuse. I felt this way because everyone else seemed strong enough to cope with the bullying.

I recently had a conversation about this school with a friend of mine and what she said was eerily true. She said it wasn't a school, it was a cult, and it had the kind of culture in which you either fit in or you didn't. There was no grey area, I didn't fit in.

I wasn't one of them. I was the one who screamed bloody murder at bullying because it was unfair, but no one else agreed with me. I recall the massive sense of immense relief I felt when my dad said, "Okay, fine. I'll be there tomorrow. I'll bring you home."

I didn't think about the consequences of my decision. All I knew was that I was getting out of that hellhole and that's all that mattered. I remember putting my suitcase on top of my bed, packing my things. I felt a sense of joy, victory and ultimate relief. However, those feelings were crushed in a single moment.

There was a group of girls close by who were gossiping. One of the girls was TWB – the one who slapped me. She was talking to her friends. I overheard them whispering to each other, "Oh, why is she leaving?" TWB retorted, "It's because people call her names." They all giggled at that, somehow finding it extremely funny. She made name calling sound normal implying I could not handle it. She made my victory seem futile.

How did I feel? Though I was victorious, they made me feel sad about my triumph and in doing so, they made me feel like I wasn't good enough...

LESSONS I LEARNT

I managed to convince my father that I needed to get out of boarding school which made me feel victorious because I succeeded in persuading him and I was finally leaving. I felt that I had somehow been rescued. However, there were people who put a dampener on my victory. They made me feel like this was nothing. I had somehow failed to go through the rite of passage.

The lesson in this for me was very simple: in life, I will be making decisions that other people will put a dampener on and even though my decisions make me happy, there will be people who try to take my happiness away from me.

One of the most important things to remember in a situation like this is that you should make decisions that make you happy. You are in charge of your own happiness. Nobody can decide what is right for you. Nobody can force you to make any decision assuming it will make you happy.

So, when people put a dampener on your decisions, and it makes you unhappy, remember one thing you are responsible for the choices you make, you are responsible for the decisions you make. More often than not, when people try to put a dampener on your happiness it's because they probably can't do what you have.

In my case, I think that everyone around me wanted to make the decision that I made. They wanted to leave the boarding school, but they didn't have the courage that I showed in making this decision. That's the key. It was courageous for me to take that stand even though I was picked on and laughed at for it.

I always try to focus on the fact that I had the courage to make such a difficult decision. But I did something unusual and unexpected which taught me that I should always focus on the courage, which is what you should do every single time you're faced with a difficult situation. When you have to make a decision which others can't accept or put a dampener on, focus on why you made that decision and remember that it takes immense courage to make difficult decisions.

EXERCISE: APPLYING THE "IT" TECHNIQUE

Coding. This is something I felt I could never learn and honestly, I never even tried to. So why am I asking you to try it? This is not coding; it is about trusting your own decisions through introspection (hence, IT). In this exercise, I want you to journal a little bit.

Think of a time when you had to make a decision that wasn't very popular. If you haven't had this experience, keep this exercise for future reference.

If you have made that difficult decision, write down:

- Why you took that decision.
- How did that decision make you feel?
- What was the end goal of that decision?

The more you can journal, the more you can understand and release those emotions, the better it is for you. Taking my example, from when I decided to leave boarding school.

- **Why did I make this decision?**

  I couldn't cope with the bullying and I figured bullying is not the way to build character. There is a better way to build character.

- **Why else did I leave boarding school?**

  Being happy is every child's right, it is every human being's right and it starts with children. I was miserable, I battled anxiety and stress day in and day out because of the environment in boarding school. This was no way for a thirteen-year-old child to live her life. A child deserves happiness and I did not have that happiness. I did not have peace of mind.

- **Why else did I make this decision?**

  I knew that there was something better than this and this was not how I was meant to live life.

And then, in conclusion:

- **How did this one decision make me feel?**

  It made me feel relieved. It felt like an immense amount of pressure was on me, weighing me down. Making this decision felt like the ropes had snapped, the boulder had rolled off and I was soaring to the surface of the water, finally taking my first deep, cleansing breath.

- **What was the end goal of that decision?**
  What was the end goal? To put an end to the bullying and the torment, if I couldn't stop it then I would re-move myself from the situation, which is exactly what I did.

It was a sense of relief, a sense of hope and a sense of joy that I would finally be able to live a life where I wouldn't feel anxious and stressed every day.

At this point, I do wish to mention that "putting an end to torment" DOES NOT entail ending your life. Speaking from a place of experience, I was told to "just die" by a certain person every time I turned to them for support. The reason I kept going to this person for support was that we are related.

Despite hearing "just die" almost daily for a year and a half, I didn't end my life because I knew the catastrophic effect it would have had on my parents. Please don't ever think that you have no other choice, you do. It is humanly impossible to have exhausted every option available. Please don't give up on yourself, you have so much to live for.

SUMMARY

- Your achievement is yours; no one can take it away from you, try as they might. When you accomplish something extremely difficult, it is a feat worth celebrating, don't allow anyone to douse the feelings of euphoria you experience.
- There will be times when the decision you take makes others unhappy. Remind yourself that it is okay, you are not responsible for making other people happy, you are responsible for making yourself happy.
- Such is life that there is always a handful of people who will never be happy or pleased with what you do, no matter how successful you become. This is their problem, their insecurities, this has nothing to do with you. Don't make this problem yours.
- The more you write out your reasons in your journal, the more reassurance you will feel within yourself.
- Ending your life is NOT AN OPTION. Ending the bullying is, ending the torment is, removing yourself from that situation is – there are countless options available, don't give up on yourself!

"I learnt that courage was not the absence of fear, but the triumph over it. The brave man is not he who does not feel afraid, but he who conquers that fear."

~ Nelson Mandela. ~

NINE: NOT GOOD ENOUGH

There are times when we feel we aren't good enough. We become judgmental towards ourselves. How do we react? How does it affect our behaviour? We start to question ourselves a lot wondering if we are on the right path.

NOT GOOD ENOUGH

When I came back from boarding school, I expected to come back to the same loving, caring, compassionate home environment that I had left behind. I didn't expect anything to have changed.

Every single time my parents had visitors come over unexpectedly, I could see their car roll up our driveway from our front window. I would tell my parents that I was going to my room. While there, I would read a book or draw, sometimes I'd write poetry or short stories.

I avoided meeting and interacting with people. I just didn't want to mingle with anyone because I felt I wasn't good enough. I felt like a failure.

The other main reason for this was that I didn't want to be asked questions like, "You're not in boarding school? How come? What happened?" I didn't want to relive the trauma I'd experienced by explaining everything I went through.

At that time, the pain was very raw and very fresh in my mind. I didn't want anyone rubbing salt on it. I was afraid that it would feel like scratching off a scab.

Back then, I felt I didn't have the strength to willingly put myself through that agony again by reliving those nightmares.

My other fear was how would people react when I told them what I went through? Would they pretend to feel sorry for me and then laugh behind my back?

I had lost my faith in people, I'd lost my faith in compassion and kindness, I genuinely felt that things like those didn't exist anymore.

I also didn't want people feeling sorry for me. More than anything, I wanted somebody to say to me, "You made the right decision, you did the right thing."

This was a far-fetched dream because no one was going to say that. But all I wanted was validation for my decision to leave boarding school, which I knew I wasn't going to get from the guests who came to visit us. It was easier to pretend that I was still away in boarding school.

In fact, I told my parents not to tell anyone that I had left boarding school and I was back at home. This continued for three months.

At the end of that term, when my brother came back from boarding school, I pretended I had returned at the same time. I went on to pretend that I had then made the decision not to go back so I wouldn't look like a quitter. I didn't want to be associated with that image.

You are probably wondering about school; how did I avoid going to school for three months?

It just worked out in my favour that at the time the schools in the area where my parents lived, were on a different school term because of which I couldn't attend school, as they were in the middle of exams and then had holidays afterward. So, it all worked out as a blessing in disguise for me that I didn't attend school.

I tried to self-study at home, but with anything that you try to do on your own, it required a lot of motivation. I was thirteen years old at the time and having self-motivation at that age is very difficult. I'm not saying it's impossible, I just couldn't do it.

It was probably because I went through so much emotional trauma which hadn't been acknowledged or validated. "Just pretend it didn't happen and move on or forget about it and move on," was all I heard myself say. It's very hard to do that because when you are suppressing emotions and you don't heal, they crop up in other forms throughout your life. This is exactly what happened to me.

I didn't attend school for three months. I hid away in my room, away from people and reality. I felt safe from prying eyes and questioning minds. In hindsight, I think it was the right thing to do because it was part of my healing process.

I wasn't emotionally ready to face anyone. I didn't want to be made to feel as if I was some sort of failure or some sort of a loser.

I'm Asian and there are high expectations of you as an Asian. You're supposed to get straight A's, you are supposed to be able to handle anything that comes your way, you are a mathematical machine.

But here I was, the anomaly of the Asian kids. I dropped out of school because I couldn't handle the bullying and I was just afraid of being judged because I didn't live up to others and societal expectations of me.

LESSONS I LEARNT

The most valuable lesson I learnt from hiding out in my room is that you shouldn't have to deal with something until you are emotionally ready. That's why I hid out in my room. I wasn't emotionally prepared to talk about the bullying that I'd faced, nor the fact that I felt like a failure for leaving boarding school at the start of the school term.

Another lesson I learnt is that we're so quick to judge what other people would think and say, but it all depends on how we explain ourselves.

At that time, I didn't have the emotional intelligence to tell whomever I could have met, had I not hidden out in my room, that this was not something I wasn't ready to talk about right at that moment, but I would when I was ready to.

However, there was always that fear of being considered a failure and at the end of the day, the world around you will perceive you as you perceive yourself. It took a very long time for me to flip that mindset, convincing myself that I wasn't a failure.

I was a very courageous person who'd taken a stand and didn't care that it was barely the start of the second school term. I didn't care that it might've messed up my education, but when it came to my emotional well-being, I made a choice.

Education can be made up. You can repeat a school year. It's not the end of the world. But if you're emotionally shattered, then that education means nothing.

Being book educated when you're not emotionally healthy is not worth it. So now, in hindsight, I see myself as a hero, because as I mentioned earlier, a friend of mine called the school a cult.

It was a cult, and I chose not to be a part of it. It took a lot of courage to turn around and say, "No, I will not put up with this."

But there were countless people who were in this cult that just quietly put up and shut up in the name of getting a good education.

Are they good, well-rounded emotional adults?

I don't know.

Do they regret not standing up for themselves?

I don't know. But I'll always encourage you to do what you feel is right for your own emotional wellbeing.

EXERCISE: APPLYING THE "FLIP THE SWITCH" TECHNIQUE

Only you get to decide that you're good enough. Isn't that such a liberating thought?

Nobody has created a set of criteria for "good enough", yet it's our perception which drags us down into this ugly and dark hole where we feel we aren't good enough.

You are as unique as your fingerprint, so, stop comparing yourself to others and feeling inadequate because of this.

A quote from Albert Einstein comes to mind here; "If you judge a fish by its ability to climb a tree, it will live its whole life believing it is stupid."

Stop judging yourself – there's no one to compare yourself to because there is no one else like you.

Enough of lecturing, let's get to work.

This is a lovely journaling exercise I do once in a while when I doubt myself so I can flip the mental switch in my mind. In your journal, write a list of all your good qualities:

- What makes you a good son/daughter?
- What makes you a good friend?
- What makes you a good sibling?
- What are your admirable personality traits?
- What are you good at?

So, if I had to make a list for myself, it would go something like this:

- My parents have always been able to count on me for anything. I've always stood by them especially during their difficult times.
- I'm a very loyal friend, I stick by my friends no matter what. It takes a lot for me to ditch a friend.
- I am a good listener. People find it easy to open up to me and often feel better after doing so.
- I am a giver, I always put others ahead of myself.

- My admirable traits are my strength and determination. A friend of mine recently said to me, "You've always had, for lack of a better word, 'guts', which means courage, but courage pales. Guts has that extra oomph and you just have this confidence, which you've always had but it is not an 'in your face' confidence. It's this confidence backed by this inner strength, that's just you."
- I am good at motivating and inspiring others. I have very strong willpower; I almost always achieve what I set out to.

I hope this example helps you trigger your own journaling and helps you identify everything that is special about you, that makes you unique and that perhaps you take for granted.

Read this every day, remind yourself of just how special you are.

Let it be your own daily dose of motivation to keep walking the path you are and trusting that you are exactly who were always meant to be.

SUMMARY

- Don't try to deal with something when you aren't emotionally ready to do so, doing so will only put you back in your healing process. But don't bottle up your feelings either, by attempting to forget everything and move on.

- The only way to move on is by healing first, not doing so leads to experiences being recycled until you learn the lesson in it for you.

- No one can tell you when you will be ready, only you know that.

- The exercise in this chapter will help start your healing process, do them as often as you need to.

- You will know you are on the right path when you start to feel better about yourself and stop questioning your value and worth.

- For additional benefits from this exercise, share it with someone you trust, preferably someone you feel close to such as a parent/grandparent/teacher/uncle/aunt, etc.

- Only you have the right to decide your worth, don't give anyone else that right and power over you.

"You are the only person you need to be good enough for."

~ Unknown. ~

TEN: HOME – PARADISE LOST

> We all make decisions expecting a certain outcome but sometimes the outcome is completely different. This can make you second guess your decisions, leading to doubts and fears.

HOME – PARADISE LOST

As I start writing this chapter, I would like to apologise to my mother because I'm sharing some intimate details of our relationship in this book. But I'm sharing this because I know that doing so will help many people.

As I mentioned earlier, when I came back home from boarding school, I was expecting to come home to that same loving and caring environment that I'd left behind. But things had changed. I felt a new kind of tension when I came back home, and I didn't quite know what it was until a few weeks later.

My mother was angry, and this hurt me deeply. I felt lonely and isolated. What was she angry about? My mom was angry that I had the courage (which is how I chose to see it) to convince my father to pull me out of boarding school. She wanted the same for my brother. She missed him and wanted him to be pulled out of boarding school too. As a mother, she missed having both her children with her and her response to the empty nest experience was anger.

Sadly, she carried a lot of anger and blame towards me that I did what my brother couldn't do. She felt it was unfair that he had to be away, and I was at home. Fact is, I don't know for sure if my brother was bullied or not. I have an inkling that he was, but he somehow found a way to cope and survive when I couldn't. I have always been someone who voiced her feelings more easily than he did.

As far as I could see it, it wasn't really my fault that he didn't try to come back from boarding school, nor that he didn't even speak to my dad about whatever he may have faced. My dad, being better and more equipped at research, made all the suggestions about the schools that we went to.

There were countless fights at home. My mom and dad kept getting into yelling matches because my mom was angry. This led me to feel angry with her because it felt like she didn't want me at home. Not that she ever said that, but that's how I perceived it.

All I remember from that time was the fights, the endless yelling and shouting. I would go to my room and close my ears, sometimes even put my head under my pillow as I had done during that pillow fight at boarding school. I remember one fight where the yelling and screaming got so bad that I couldn't take it anymore.

I walked up to them and fell to my knees, plugged my ears with my forefingers, and screamed at the top of my lungs, "Please just stop! Please just stop!" I was screaming and crying.

It was incidents like these that made me doubt myself and my decision to leave boarding school. Obviously, it was causing a lot of tension and a lot of friction in the house. I blamed myself for creating this situation at home. I remember being mad at myself for causing this, and at my mom for not being happy to have me at home. All I wanted was that loving, compassionate and caring environment that I had left behind.

I didn't get that when I came back home, there was just so much stress. I didn't have my brother close by to talk to about this. These were the days before cell phone technology, so I would've had to have made an international call to speak to him, and either way, I didn't want to stress him out, either.

So as a child, I was holding all these emotions inside and feeling like the centre of blame for all the unhappiness in what was once a loving home. And it was a lot for a child who was bullied to take on. Dealing with trying to overcome the emotional scars of bullying and then dealing with the tension in what was once my safe haven was really hard, and the anger didn't lead to healthy behaviours at all.

LESSONS I LEARNT

The most profound lesson I learnt through this experience was that the grass isn't always greener on the other side. But sometimes you have to choose the lesser of two evils, which is what I did. I chose to leave boarding school where I was being emotionally and sometimes physically battered to come home to emotional tension.

The difference was that the emotional tension at home wasn't an everyday occurrence; it happened once every couple of days at most. And because both of my parents worked all day, I only needed to deal with the unease in the evenings or weekends. I could cope with that.

The other lesson I learnt is that sometimes when we make decisions, the people we expect to support us the most, don't. It can be very disappointing. It makes us question ourselves and the big decision we made.

Again, I'm going to tell you to trust your instincts because if you don't believe in yourself, and in the strength of what you decided to do, nobody else will. You won't be able to convince anyone around you if you're not convinced yourself. So, focus on the lesser of two evils, because sometimes you have to make those sorts of decisions. After which, you can focus on ways to cope amidst your new circumstances.

EXERCISE: APPLYING THE "PPP" TECHNIQUE

Have you ever looked at the picture on postcard closely? It is perfect; hence, we have the picture-perfect postcard technique in which you share how you feel fearlessly – in a picture-perfect postcard way! In this specific exercise, I want to focus on being able to communicate how you feel with somebody who isn't happy with the decision that you have made.

Now, it depends on the person and whether they matter to you or not. In my case, it was my mom, and she matters to me. So, if I could have written this letter back then, I would have. I also understand that you, as a teenager, might not necessarily have the vocabulary nor the emotional maturity yet to write things like this. So, I'm giving you an example of what you can say for you to write your own letter.

My letter to my mother would have said things like,

"I understand that you wish my brother had left boarding school just as I did, but I cannot control his decisions. Please try to understand that if I'd continued to stay in that boarding school, I would've had a mental breakdown and I am sure that's not what you want for your daughter. You'd want her to be safe, secure and happy. So please, can you help me find that safety, security and comfort that I need right now, here at home? Please accept this decision that I have taken even though you may not like it. Remember, I am your child and I need your support. I cannot heal without your support."

It's these things that you need to put in a letter if the person matters to you, and if your decision has upset this person. Keep it very simple.

SAMPLE LETTER

(to someone you care about explaining your decision which has made them unhappy)

Hi _____ *(insert name of the person you are writing to)*

I know you are upset with me and if I were in your shoes, I would be upset with me too but please hear me out *(the reason for this sentence is to validate how they feel, once you validate how someone feels, they tend to be more open to hearing you out).*

I know that my decision to _____ *(insert the decision you took)* has disappointed you. I want you to know that I am sorry for upsetting you, but I also want you to know why I took this decision. I am sure once you hear my reasoning for it, you won't be as upset with me.

I took this decision because _____ *(list out every reason why you took this decision - I have a separate exercise on this about writing down your "why's" for your decision, use that exercise to complete this letter). Sign off this letter in a way that best describes you and your personality.*

SUMMARY

- Some decisions leave us at a crossroads, wondering if we did the right thing. More often than not, it's a case of choosing the lesser of two evils because one is more manageable than the other.

- Don't beat yourself up if you find yourself in such a situation. You did what you thought was best and it's definitely better than not doing anything at all.

- Don't allow your current circumstances to define the rest of your life.

- Communication is the key, sometimes we may "talk", but we fail to "communicate". We "hear" but we don't "listen" and worse yet, we hear only to answer, not to understand.

My own experience taught me that I had the courage to make a difficult decision even though I wasn't as happy as I could have been, at least I wasn't being bullied anymore. Sometimes, it is a case of picking the lesser of two evils, "better the devil you know than the devil you don't."

"Learn how to ask for what you need in a way that leaves your community feeling not only empowered to give you what you ask for but inspired to do so."

~ Lisa Nichols. ~

ELEVEN: BAD HABITS

Have you ever developed any "unhealthy habits" to stifle your emotions? Simply because it is easier to nurture this habit than it is to face the reality of what you are battling within? I did. I couldn't face my emotions, so I stifled them - with food.

BAD HABITS

If you recall, I mentioned earlier that not dealing with my emotions led to an unhealthy habit, and this is exactly what I am sharing with you in this chapter. I had what now might be called Binge-Eating Disorder. No, it wasn't anything like the usual eating disorders you hear about, like anorexia or bulimia. I did, however, stuff down my emotions with food.

Remember how I always used to hide out in my room whenever we had guests come over, and how I was home alone all day because both my parents were at work?

These were the occasions when I would indulge in not-so-healthy snacks. Anything that was high in sugar, high in salt and lots of carbs. I was stuffing my face. Was I hungry? No, but I ate to comfort myself. I ate to stifle my emotions.

I ate because it was easier to eat than it was to let the tears spill over. I was dealing with the fact that I took a decision that made me look like a failure in the eyes of my parents, even though they didn't say it.

Coming from the kind of culture that I do and living in a community surrounded by overachieving Asians, the fact that my brother and I were away in boarding school was something to be proud of, something to be bragged about. Yet, here I was, after quitting everything and returning home, defeated and dejected.

Dealing with those emotions wasn't easy. Nobody said anything to me. It's not that my parents accused me of being a failure nor did they berate me for what I saw as taking a bad decision. It was how I felt and how I saw myself.

So rather than cry and then try to explain my tears to anyone, I found it easier to stifle my emotions with food.

Often, we had guests visit us, and stay for hours. I would ask my mom for snacks, telling her that I didn't want to skip dinner because of the extended stay of the guests. So, I ended up eating alone in my room, because the guests would stay for so long that my parents would offer them a meal. They'd eat together, laughing and joking whilst I hid out in my room, reading a book or writing. I tried drawing pictures to distract myself, but it was always food that I needed around. It was easier to focus on the food than it was on the emotions and the reasons why I was alone in my room.

Naturally, at thirteen years old, I was a growing child and the effects of eating unhealthy foods started to show. I was no longer as slender as I used to be.

I remember when my brother came back from boarding school for spring break, we went away on vacation to a city called Durban in South Africa.

It was hotter than I'd expected it to be and my parents eased up on their conservative ways about my dressing, so they were okay with it if I chose to wear shorts to the beach. Because I didn't own any, I borrowed a pair from my brother and they actually fit me. My brother is two years older than I am, and obviously, as a boy, he's built differently compared to me. But I filled out the shorts - by no means were they loose on me.

Our hotel was on the beachfront with steps leading down to the beach. On one particular day when we were heading back to the hotel, I was walking ahead up the flight of stairs and my mom was behind me.

That's when she commented on how I had filled out.

Though she tried to put it as gently as possible, the implication was that I had gained a significant amount of weight. I knew it was due to the unhealthy snacking I'd taken on to avoid dealing with my emotions.

As well as not being able to convey exactly how I was feeling, I think what made it really hard was the lack of validation I'd experienced. I felt that even if I tried to explain myself, no one would say, "We understand how you feel. How can we help you?"

That's all it would've taken. Just two simple sentences. My fear of not getting those two sentences of validation kept me from talking about how I felt, and I ended up making unhealthy decisions that affected my health and made me feel uncomfortable in my own skin.

LESSONS I LEARNT

The most important lesson I learnt through this disordered eating was that there are better ways to deal with hurt and pain. The only thing you achieve when you bottle up your emotions in any way is punishing yourself.

We assume that the people around us won't understand how we feel. But the problem with that assumption is that we lose out. We won't know unless we try. My biggest thing was that I felt terribly alone. I felt a lack of support from my parents, because I think they were dealing with their own stress about the situation and they didn't know how to help me.

At the end of the day, I realise that if I had just tried to communicate with them, sharing my feelings about everything, and told them how much I needed their support, perhaps things would've been different. Another issue was that I didn't really know what kind of support I actually needed. The implication of everyone's silence was simple - you're no longer in that situation so forget about it, no point in digging up old wounds. The best way to heal is to forget about it and move on.

However, the most important part of forgetting what happened to you is being able to let it go. Otherwise, all you're doing is suppressing it, which is what I did by eating all that food.

I suspect that even if my parents asked me to talk about it, I wouldn't have been able to. Perhaps all I needed was a little extra love and compassion but as a teenager, I felt awkward asking for it. It's hard as a teenager to ask for that extra love because it feels weird; you're still a kid who wants that love, but you desperately want to be semi-grown up.

EXERCISE: APPLYING THE "BBB" TECHNIQUE

Let's talk about the "Break the Bad Behaviour" technique. Has there ever been a time in your life when you have taken on an unhealthy habit to deal with stress, anxiety or emotional turmoil? It can be something as simple as biting your nails or something more drastic, like when I stuffed down my emotions with food.

What can you do about this? I'd suggest journaling. First journal about your emotions. What emotions are you dealing with right now? And why are these emotions so powerful over you?

Sometimes just identifying what upsets you, empowers you. Knowledge is power after all.

The next step is to list out replacement habits that you can consider. For example, it was many years later when I realised the joy I got from any physical activity - like running or playing badminton. It helped me release stress and I started doing that more and more. Badminton was my go-to sport every time I was hurt or angry.

Much later, I learnt that exercise releases endorphins which make you feel happy. So, think of activities that give you a good feeling about yourself. It can be anything creative such as drawing or painting, or it can be playing a game of basketball, dodgeball, badminton or tennis.

Actively seek and try out different healthy habits until you figure out what makes you happy then replace your unhealthy habits with these healthy habits. Give yourself at least ten days of trying out a new habit to replace the unhealthy one. If, after ten days of trying the new habit, you don't like it, move on to the next one. But the focus should be on replacing the unhealthy habit and journaling about it. The more action you take and the more you take note of the action, the more empowered you will feel.

I would recommend meditation as well. But then again, it's very, very hard for a wandering mind to meditate. It's always worth a try though. Start with something simple, a ten-minute meditation to help you calm your emotions down. See if this works for you.

SUMMARY

- It's easy to fall into a victim mentality, especially when we don't communicate how we feel.
- Communication is the key to healing. Just knowing that you *always* have a choice, even when it doesn't feel like you do, is comforting on its own.
- Not making a decision is a decision in itself - recognise that.
- You can always choose healthier habits to replace the unhealthy ones. Healing starts with one positive step after the other.
- When we write things down, it brings our sub-conscious thoughts into our conscious minds which in turn helps us become aware of our thoughts and actions. When we are aware of our actions, it empowers us to choose wisely.
- Never forget that you always, always have the power to choose.

"People are more comfortable with familiar discomfort than they are with an unfamiliar new possibility"

~ Lisa Nichols. ~

TWELVE: BECOMING WHAT I DESPISED

> *What happens when you become the very thing you detest? And worse, you don't even realise when and how it happened? I became a bully of sorts, and there was a lesson in it for me which I hope you can learn as well.*

BECOMING WHAT I DESPISED

After spending three months at home waiting for the new school term to start, I finally went back to school. I only attended the new school for three months until the end of the school year, after which I transferred to another one closer to home. Because this was a "better" school, they didn't do mid-year admissions, so I had to wait for the new year to start.

I made a few friends. Some of them were people I knew from before going away to boarding school, that I'd met when we first moved to South Africa. I was slowly beginning to settle. The school days were very long, though. I remember being in school from around 7:30 AM to 4:00 PM. We would have school all morning and then we'd have study sessions in the afternoons to help prepare for exams. The school did this to secure first place in the national twelfth-grade results. This was the only way to ensure that kids didn't avoid studying if they went home. Unfortunately, these sessions were compulsory.

I can't quite pinpoint when and how this happened, but I became a little bit of a bully.

I don't mean I was like the girls that taunted and hit me in boarding school, but that doesn't make it any better. I would play one friend off against the other. I'd be nice to one and speak badly to the other about the former. It was only silly things like this, but it's still no excuse.

I also used a lot of swear words then, because it made me feel powerful and I thought I'd get away with it. But the student that I swore at told the principal and I was called into her office for using offensive language.

I was told to apologise and to guarantee that I wouldn't repeat that offense again. This just angered me, because I remembered being beaten up for calling someone out on swearing and here I was, doing the exact same thing. I found it unfair; I didn't get the privilege that my bully did when I was in boarding school.

But this didn't stop my behaviour. I stopped swearing, but I didn't stop playing one friend against the other, nor did I treat anyone with basic respect.

Honestly, this didn't make me feel good. By no means did I feel wonderful about what I was doing. But it gave me a sense of power and control. After leaving boarding school, one of the things I really struggled with was feeling in control of what's going on around me. I felt powerless.

I wanted my words and my actions to matter, I wanted to be heard, but this was the wrong way of going about it. Perhaps it enabled me to understand why bullies bully.

Hurt people hurt people.

You can only give what you have. If all you have is hurt, then that is all you are going to give. I fell into the same trap that my bullies had fallen into. I don't know what their situation was, but I do know that normal people do not go around breaking other people down.

As lame as it may sound, I realised that I was behaving horribly just so that I could feel that I existed, that I was important, that my voice mattered and that my feelings were important. This was all a culmination of the lack of power and validation I'd felt both at boarding school and after I'd left. Suddenly I just had to pick up the pieces and move on as if nothing had happened. But something did happen, and it broke me down inside. No one was willing to acknowledge this, and I had to carry on as nothing had happened.

How do you do that? My response to the anger and pain I felt inside of me became the anger and hurt I inflicted on others around me.

But this is not the answer.

Trust me, this is my voice of experience speaking; this really isn't the way to go. Following this path didn't make me feel good. It might've made me feel temporarily powerful, but then I started alienating my friends and I became isolated because no one really wanted to be associated with me afterward. This wasn't a nice feeling. I'd become a horrible person just to have a sense of power or control, and I lost friends in the process.

What I'm trying to explain here is that when I was being bullied, I felt that my bullies were superior to me. Once I realised that my bullies weren't better than me and were probably dealing with a whole lot more crap than I was, it made me feel normal. It made me feel like there was nothing wrong with me at all. This was an amazing realisation for me.

LESSONS I LEARNT

I realised that no one is born a bully, our circumstances either make or break us. Whether my bullies understood this or not, it didn't matter. But I learnt that you can't build something positive out of negative behaviour.

You may feel powerful temporarily, but that power isn't worth the isolation and misery you feel afterward. Bullies are nothing but hurt people. It doesn't justify what they do to others, but at least it makes you, as a victim, realise that there is nothing wrong with you, that you did not do anything to bring the bullying behaviour upon yourself. You didn't do anything to deserve this.

Once you recognise that your bully is just someone who's hurting, it becomes easier for you to forgive yourself as a victim of bullying. Somewhere along the line, I blamed myself for bringing this bullying upon myself, I felt that I did something to attract it to myself, or I deserved it somehow. But it gave me the opportunity as a victim of bullying, to start forgiving myself and to start accepting and respecting myself just the way I was.

This experience also helped me realise the sort of person I didn't want to be. It made me realise that I have a choice. We always have a choice. We don't have to become what people do to us. I had to make a decision: either I become that victim who is hurting and in turn hurting others, or I become somebody who chooses not to do to others what was done to her.

EXERCISE: APPLYING THE "3 I'S AND A T" TECHNIQUE

We will get to the name later, let's start our work first. This is going to be a three-part exercise.

1. Identify incidents when you might have done something which was borderline bullying or even bullying itself.
2. Forgive yourself.
3. Apologise.

If you've never done anything that was borderline bullying or even bullying, then skip to exercise two.

Part one

I would like you to journal about any given time when you might've said something mean or nasty to someone, not necessarily as a way of defending yourself, but perhaps to fit in. Ask yourself:

- Why did you do that?
- What was the goal behind doing that?
- Was it because everyone else was doing it?
- Or was there another reason why you did it?
- How did it make you feel afterward?

The point of this exercise is to identify your feelings. As I've mentioned before, your feelings are your compass, they will guide you to make the right decision. If something doesn't make you feel good or proud or confident, you shouldn't be doing it. By all means, stand up for yourself, but do it without being mean.

Part two

Forgive yourself. This may sound silly, but I cannot even begin to emphasise the importance of forgiving yourself - whether you're a victim of bullying or a bully.

If you're a victim, remember, you aren't what happened to you, but you are what you make of what happened to you. As a victim of bullying, I always felt there was something wrong with me, that I somehow deserved to be bullied.

Forgiving yourself helps you consciously recognise that it wasn't your fault, you may know this subconsciously, but it's important to validate this in your own conscious mind.

For the process of forgiving yourself, we will apply the "3 I's and T" technique. I want you to stand in front of a mirror, look yourself in the eye and say these words three times:

- I am sorry.
- I forgive you.
- I love you.
- Thank you.

What are you sorry for? Sorry for believing that there was something wrong with you, sorry for believing that you brought this upon yourself (as a victim of bullying). Sorry for making an unwise choice (as a bully).

What are you forgiving yourself for? Exactly the same things – believing there was something wrong with you, that you brought this upon yourself or for making an unwise choice.

I love you – this is self-explanatory. Love, respect, dignity – it all starts with you. You get to show others how to treat you based on how you treat yourself.

Thank you? Thank yourself for apologising, for forgiving yourself and for loving yourself.

Part three

Apologising to whom you've hurt, if you so did as a bully. This is hard and you should only do this if you feel comfortable enough to do so.

Often, people don't react the way you expect them to. If you cannot directly apologise to the person you hurt then practice it privately, not in front of a mirror but with conscious thoughts of the person you hurt.

The next best thing you can do after this is to change your behaviour towards this person. You don't have to become their BFF, but you can treat them with dignity and respect. Plant that seed and nurture it with kindness. I guarantee it will bring you so much happiness.

SUMMARY

- You can only give what you have. Granted, it's a choice, but for a young mind, it's extremely difficult to make that choice when it seems easier to lash out.

- Remember, we always have the power of our choices - something I learnt the hard way.

- Once we realise the power we have by choosing which path to take, it's the most liberating feeling one can experience.

- The more you practice the exercises in this chapter, the better you will feel about yourself as a person.

- Don't hesitate to repeat the exercises over and over until you reap the true benefits of them.

- Always remember that it is okay to make mistakes, as long you learn from them and as long as you don't repeat them.

- Forgiving yourself is key, don't keep beating yourself up about the past, choose to see the past as an opportunity to grow.

"I am not a product of my circumstances. I am a product of my decisions."

~ Stephen Covey. ~

THIRTEEN: THE MEETING – BEING HEARD FOR THE FIRST TIME

> *What does victory feel like? For me, it was like coming up for air after being submerged underwater for an extended amount of time. It felt like I'd finally been noticed, and my voice was heard for the very first time.*

THE MEETING - BEING HEARD FOR THE FIRST TIME

After about a year and a half of being at home and attending a local school, I realised that it was time for me to move. I wasn't happy at home and it wasn't fun without my brother there. I seemed to be bearing the brunt of a lot of tension, which I felt was unfair on me.

But the main issue was that I wasn't getting a good enough education and exposure to sports the way I wanted to. I was subjected to corporal (or physical) punishment twice in the year I was at this particular school. Once was on my knuckles - three strikes with the back of a blackboard duster - and the other time was on the palm on my hand - three strikes with a cut off hosepipe.

Twice may not seem like a lot but it was brutal punishment which left me swollen and bruised. It was humiliating because the punishment was given out in front of other students, who laughed at my expense. I didn't want to learn this way. Surely there was a better way to learn.

I was halfway through grade eleven when I told my parents that I wanted to go away to another boarding school. So, my father started researching, and he found two all-girls boarding schools in Johannesburg, which was about a six-hour drive from where my parents lived at the time.

It wasn't too far away, and it was in the same country, unlike my previous boarding school. We didn't have to worry about getting through customs and passport control or visas.

My father sent over my latest transcripts and grades to the two different schools along with all the application forms. It was the middle of the school year, so I was expected to write entrance exams and go through an interview process to be selected or declined admission.

When I went to both schools for the entrance exams and interviews, I immediately preferred one school over the other, but I was declined admission to that school because I didn't perform as well in the exam. They felt my math skills weren't up to par according to their expectations.

So, I ended up getting into the school which was my second choice.

I remember the day I was supposed to go away to boarding school again. I was nervous, but I packed my things. I had my school uniform and everything I needed, and we drove the six hours to the school. When we got there, I was tired from the drive, but I was asked to meet with the principal and the vice-principal before I settled into the boarding house.

When I got to the meeting, a huge disappointment awaited me. In no way was I prepared for this. I learnt that they'd put me back a year; I was halfway through grade eleven in my old school, and the new one had put me in grade ten. Their reasoning for this was that I was too young to be in grade eleven. I was fifteen at that time and according to them, the acceptable age for grade eleven was a minimum of sixteen.

I remember sitting there feeling very angry and frustrated. I felt like I was being forced to do something that was very unfair on me and I had no choice. This decision had been made for me, without my permission. I was faced with unfairness, yet again.

I struggled to keep my emotions in check. I was very close to tears; my eyes were stinging as I desperately blinked back the tears as best as I could. I just sat there, looking down initially as I gathered my thoughts. I finally plucked up the courage and with a trembling voice, I asked to share my thoughts on their decision. I got into a debate with the principal and vice principal.

In the most respectful way that I could, I told them that I understood their concerns about my age. However, I had already passed grade ten and my marks were proof of it. I told them that I felt it was very unfair of them to put me back a grade just because of my age. I told them that they were failing me without even giving me a chance. The marks I'd obtained when I passed grade ten was proof enough that I knew the subject matter of that grade enough to have cleared my exams.

Though I was very upset, I kept my emotions in check as I calmly requested them not to put me back a year - it would be very discouraging for me, and that wasn't the best way for me to start my learning at a new school.

I remember them looking at each other, back and forth just wondering what to do next. They probably didn't expect this from me. The principal picked up the grade eleven class lists and started going through them. At the time, I didn't know what they were looking at, I just held my breath as no one said anything.

I felt my heart leap when the principal said, "Well, our grade eleven classes are all full. We'll see where we can find a spot for you."

I couldn't believe that they'd accepted my argument, my side of the story. And guess what? They managed to find a spot in one of the grade eleven classes! I was deeply grateful. I thanked them profusely even though I was trembling inside with excitement and release of fear. My legs were wobbly when I walked out of there and I recall that my father turned around, looked at me and he said to me, "I'm really proud of you."

"I am proud of you for the way you handled that." Growing up, I am sure my father must've told me countless times before how proud of me he was, but that was one time I distinctly remember because I no longer felt like a loser. I'd achieved something that was proud-worthy.

LESSONS I LEARNT

This one experience taught me that my voice mattered, so long as I communicated how and what I felt in an effective way. I had to use logical arguments and emotions that mattered specifically in that situation – being passionate without losing my temper.

Since then, every time I've needed to communicate something important that matters to me, I use the same technique. It was the perfect opportunity for me to learn how to use my voice in a way that I got my message across.

It taught me that I've always had a voice that mattered. It was the way I was conveying this voice that didn't give me the results that I wanted. Not only that, but the lack of expressing how I truly felt worked against me. I just assumed people would understand how I felt because they could see I was suffering but people aren't mind readers. Until you start openly sharing how you feel in a clear, concise, emotionally intelligent way, you won't start seeing the results you want.

EXERCISE: APPLYING THE "LOUDSPEAKER" TECHNIQUE

Grab a megaphone for this technique! Just kidding! This is a journaling and letter writing exercise. I want you to journal about a time when you needed something, and you were able to communicate it effectively, versus a time when you needed something and you were unable to communicate it effectively.

Think of incidents throughout your life and see what was different about the two situations. Did you struggle to communicate properly what you wanted when you didn't get what you want? And what about the times when you did get what you want? What was different about the way you communicated your desires and your wants?

Take note of this. When it comes to communicating effectively what you want; whether it is changing your school or wanting to be home-schooled because of bullying, write your points of argument down so you can communicate without getting frustrated.

Be very, very clear on why you wish to study from home or change your school. If you don't know how to communicate how you feel, then refer to some of the other letter samples I've given to you and grab the feelings from there and write it down. Explain to whomever you may need to convince how you feel and leave it in their hands, trusting that whatever happens is in your best interests because there is no lack of effort from your side.

SUMMARY

- We all have a voice that matters. More often than not, it's how we choose to communicate our feelings that derail our train resulting in frustration of not being heard.
- Using the guidelines I've provided, see if it makes a difference in helping people understand you.
- Take note of what works for you personally from the exercises and what doesn't. Practice more and more of what works for you as often as you need to.
- After this, your voice will no longer remain a whisper.

"I have learnt over the years that when one's mind is made up, this diminishes fear; knowing what must be done does away with fear."

~ Rosa Parks. ~

FOURTEEN: MY SILVER LINING

> *These are stories of kindness that I experienced during that harrowing year and a half in boarding school. The purpose of sharing these stories is to inspire you to consciously look for those who are kind to you. Recognise them, acknowledge and appreciate them.*

MY SILVER LINING

Despite everything I had faced, I can't deny the fact that there were many who were very kind to me during my time at boarding school. Though they couldn't stop the bullying, they offered me comfort, companionship and acceptance. After all, isn't that what we all want? To be accepted the way we are without being judged for it.

(*Names changed to protect privacy.)

A lovely senior called Henry* was a tall, lanky guy who always smiled at me. He'd always invite me to sit with his friends without worrying about being teased or targeted by my bullies for choosing to be my friend. On an especially dark, rainy day - the weather reflecting my mood - he picked a flower for me to cheer me up. I never saw it in a romantic way nor was it intended that way; it was a caring gesture from a kind friend, an act that made me feel less lonely.

A friend and classmate, Ella*, was exactly what you'd picture if you think of an angel. She had the voice of a nightingale, when she sang, we all fell silent and were mesmerised. I often felt she was "cool" and "popular" because she had such an incredible talent and gift. Yet, she chose to be my friend risking her popularity by hanging out with me - someone who was considered weird by most.

On sports day, I was participating in the Shot-Put competition. I wasn't good, but I could at least participate. There were about five girls, and many of them were a lot bigger and stronger than I was. However, I managed to win that specific event. I came first! I was the one who threw the ball the farthest!

Ella was the one who was cheering the loudest for me. I remember when I ran over to her to share what I had achieved, she had already heard the announcement over the PA system that I was the first. She was jumping up and down in sheer excitement. She hugged me tight and kept saying over and over, "Oh my God. Oh, my God. You won. You won!" It felt so lovely to have somebody cheer me on so passionately and love me so dearly

There was a senior called Penelope* who always had so much love and compassion. She saw the sadness in my eyes, and she tried her best to comfort me. Every time I walked past with sullen look on my face, she would invite me to sit with her and ask her friends to join us. She did everything she could to make me feel accepted. I used to have so much fun hanging out with them and talking to them because they were interested in what I had to say. They were very caring people. I slowly started opening up about the bullying to Penelope and her friends.

I remember one day things got to this point where she had enough of my suffering, and she wanted to do something for me. She walked back with me to the boarding house and she gathered all the students there, all the juniors.

She ripped into them, saying, "This is enough. You will not hurt this girl anymore. It is not nice to be mean to others. How would you feel if someone was mean to you?" She stood up for me. She showed me that I was worthy of standing up for and I felt so loved and so respected in that one instance, in that one deed she did for me. I felt wonderful that someone cared enough about what I was feeling and that my feelings mattered enough to act.

Another incredible friend worth mentioning is Hannah*, a beautiful person inside and out who always had compassion. She never participated in any bullying towards me. She was always interested in what I had to say and took the time to spend time with me and talk to me.

In fact, she was the one who told me the meaning of the names I was called - Sis Mary and Sis Georgina. It seemed as though those words hurt her as deeply as they hurt me. She was a person who always showed kindness no matter what. I learnt much later on that she was also bullied. Perhaps that's why she was so kind to me – she knew what it felt like. I'm proud to say that to this day, we have remained very, very good friends.

Rylee* was another girl who was always kind to me, who always had comforting words. Every time I was crying after being bullied, she always had a hug for me, every time I was homesick, she held me until all the tears ran out. She also never participated in any of the bullying directed at me.

Another lovely friend I would like to mention is Mary*. She was another very kind soul, and someone I'm still friends with today thanks to social media, even though we reconnected many years later.

I'll never forget my 12th birthday. It was my first birthday away from home and naturally, I was homesick and missing my parents.

Mary got her mother to bake a chocolate cake for me, for my birthday. Though Mary was in boarding school, her family lived nearby – but not close enough for the daily commute to and from school, so she spent weekdays in boarding school and weekends at home.

The cake her mother baked was the most delicious cake I've ever had. She organized a little birthday party for me to make me feel better and it was the sweetest thing anyone had ever done for me at that time. There were treats and snacks and of course, there was the chocolate cake. There were probably only about four or five of us at my party, but it was so much fun because of the kind gesture shown to me.

Most importantly, it helped me not miss my parents as much on my birthday.

I believe all these friends who stood by and watched as I was bullied have dealt with some guilt of not being able to do anything because they didn't want to be victimised. They would have been bullied too. However, knowing what the effects of bullying felt like, they always had love, compassion and comfort to offer me afterward.

When I decided to write this book, the memories of those who were kind to me all came flooding back. I remembered almost every single individual's name even after thirty years. As a firm believer in expressing gratitude, I reached out to as many of them as I could, finding them on Facebook, asking mutual friends to assist me in connecting with them so that I could thank them.

What do you really say when you reach out to someone after thirty years, when you're not sure if they even remember you? Well, my emails went something like this:

"Hey! I'm not sure if you remember me or not, but you were my senior at boarding school. I will never forget the kindness you showed me as I was bullied throughout my short time at the school.

Thank you for your kindness. I remember that, at a time when being cool and popular was so important, you chose to be kind. You always invited me to sit with you and your friends, making me feel included at a time when I was isolated by others. You always had a smile and a kind word to encourage me. You valued being kind far more than you valued being popular - that is huge and highly commendable especially at a time when things like kindness wasn't openly discussed nor taught in schools."

And the responses I got went something like this

"Hi, Kalyani. I do remember you but have to admit I don't remember what happened. Thank you so much for reaching out. I am very touched by your message but feel a heaviness to know you had such a tough time. Thank you for finding me and thank you for your kind words."

And some like this:

"Oh my goodness, this has brought tears to my eyes! I want to thank you for reminding me all these years later how we can affect each other. Thank you. I'm glad that the younger me did whatever she did and made you feel how you felt."

And others like this:

"Hi there.

I'm so sorry that you went through that. Can't say I remember exactly but your face looks very familiar to me.

Thank you for reaching out and for sharing your story. It's bloody shameful what happened there - and so many of us were blind to the pain that was all around us... sigh... Now my eldest is thirteen and about to enter high school. I think I will give her your story to read and hope that she can make a difference in someone's life."

LESSONS I LEARNT

I don't know if you've ever done an experiment as a kid, where you try to burn a piece of paper with the focal point of a magnifying glass. This is how we often respond during difficult times, we focus only on the problem and not on anything else around us.

It took me years to understand the lesson in this experience. It was quite simple actually - no matter what a rough time you may be going through, there are always people who care about you. There's always kindness around you. There was always light at the end of the tunnel, and it's not an oncoming train. The problem is that we tend to focus so much on our misery and what is making us miserable and on our problems that we tend to ignore what's good in our lives.

No matter how hard things are, there's always something to be grateful for. And you don't have to wait for Thanksgiving to be grateful. You can be grateful right here and right now. All it takes is the right perception and opening your mind and eyes to see the blessings. I truly believe that there is always a blessing. There is always a lesson in everything. And even though I was going through such a difficult time, I had more than a handful of people who cared about me, were kind to me, who had compassion for me, who would listen to me. However, at that time, I was so focused on the people who made me miserable that I couldn't see the kind people

It took so many years for me to see this and even though I eventually did reach out to thank them, it took me a long time to do so. Don't take as long as I did.

EXERCISE: APPLYING THE "MAGNIFYING GLASS" TECHNIQUE

It is all about what you focus on, so let us refocus our magnifying glass. This will be a two-part exercise. The first involves journaling, and the second is a letter writing one.

In your journal, write out the names of people who you feel have been kind to you and the acts of kindness they have shown to you. This might be easy, or it may require a bit of soul searching, but make the effort to identify and recognise the people who have been kind to you whilst you have been bullied. Whether it's a friend, a teacher, a counsellor, or someone else, write their names down.

The second part of this exercise is writing a message to them to say thank you. It can be an email, a text, a card or a letter - whatever is most comfortable for you.

The point of this exercise is to show gratitude because the more you are grateful, the more you will have to be grateful for.

SAMPLE LETTER

(To those who have shown you kindness in your darkest hour)

Hi _____

I thought to reach out to say thank you. I really appreciate what you did for me when I was being bullied. *(Insert what they did for you in as much detail as possible, the more detail, the better because it shows how much their gesture meant to you that you remember every detail of it).*

You gave me hope when I felt there was none, you showed me that there was nothing wrong with me, you showed me that I was "good enough" through your act of kindness. Thank you for being who you are and for spreading kindness where you go. Thank you for making a difference in my dark day.

(Sign off this message in a way that best describes you and your personality).

SUMMARY

- When trudging through a tough time, we are so focused on what's going wrong that we totally miss out on everything that's going right in our lives.
- The purpose of sharing these experiences with you is to enable you to shift your focus away from the hurt and agony to the kind acts of others. Don't wait too long to do this, do it now.
- Repeat these exercises as often as you need to. More often than not, you may find that those you validate actually needed that validation.

"Too many people miss the silver lining because they are expecting gold."

~ Maurice Setter. ~

FIFTEEN: WHAT KEEPS YOU UP AT NIGHT?

When I announced on social media that I intended to write this book, I was encouraged by so many people that I asked the general public to send me their burning questions about bullying. Some of the questions came from parents and some from teenagers - feel free to read this with your parents, perhaps some of their questions might be answered, too.

ANSWERING YOUR BURNING QUESTIONS ON BULLYING

Why do parents of most bullies refuse to acknowledge their child's behaviour and take action?

There are a number of reasons for this. I think a lot of parents are in denial that their child is capable of such emotionally destructive behaviour. Somewhere along the line, the parents are in denial that they raised a bully - because no one is born a bully. Parents refuse to take responsibility for that kind of behaviour. Sometimes, bullying behaviour starts at home, when a child is being bullied by their parents or by other kids in their neighbourhood.

In order to acknowledge that their child is a bully, the parents need to acknowledge that somehow, somewhere along the line, they are responsible for this.

And one of the most difficult things to do is to admit that you are at fault. Everyone takes it on their ego and takes it very personally.

How do bullies choose their victims?

Honestly, from my own personal experience, it's trial and error. I believe bullies just pick on anyone and then continue to bully those who struggle to stand up for themselves.

I was an easy target because I didn't know how to stand up for myself. I moved to South Africa during the peak of apartheid and my parents told me in no uncertain terms that I did not have the right skin colour to have a say in the country we moved to, so it was best for me if I kept a low profile. In doing so, I ended up becoming a very easy target for my bullies.

But in cases not related to race or other discrimination, I would feel that the victim is chosen by a bully randomly, a trial and error process. They keep trying until they find that one person who is not going to kick up enough of a storm for the bully to be severely punished. So, remember, it's not your fault. You didn't do anything to bring this upon yourself. Please don't blame yourself.

Why does a bully, bully?

I can't say it enough; hurt people hurt people. You can only give what you have. If all you have is hurt and agony, that's all you're going to give to others. No, this doesn't make it right, it does not justify what they are doing to you. I say this with conviction because I truly believe we have a choice in every situation. If we are hurting, we can respond to it the way we choose to, in a healthy way, instead of hurting others.

When we know being hurt ourselves does not feel good, how can hurting others feel good, it wouldn't make any sense to do so. Happy people don't hurt other people.

That said, it's very important to understand that bullies lash out because they feel helpless. It gives them a sense of control and power against whatever they're battling. It is not right. But in understanding this, I think we begin to learn that as a victim of bullying, we are not at fault.

Do the victims of bullying and the parents of these victims feel that the school is doing enough to put an end to bullying?

No, absolutely not. If the school was doing enough, there wouldn't be so many anti-bullying campaigns. If it was nipped in the bud right from the start, there wouldn't be a need for any of this, this book that I'm writing and the countless workshops that are out there as well as other books that are out there on bullying. So, something needs to be done that is effective, and that will work but it will take time to figure out what that is.

How do we teach young kids about bullying?

I think one of the most important lessons we need to learn no matter what age we are, is self-respect. We need to respect ourselves enough to draw the line when it comes to behaviour towards us, behaviour that makes us uncomfortable, that makes us uneasy and unhappy. You should respect yourself enough not to tolerate any kind of mean behaviour towards you. It starts with understanding what self-respect is and understanding what your own personal boundaries are.

There are times when people joke around and that's okay to a certain extent but once it starts hurting you, that's when you need to take a step back and say, "No, I don't like this."

One of the best examples I can give you is pranking. I'm often asked why I don't like pranking other people or being pranked myself. This is because I find it hurtful. For me, jokes should be laughed at, not people. But that's my personal opinion. You're welcome to disagree with it

What can we do to prevent a child from being bullied?

Self-awareness. I think it's so important that schools and parents teach children to be self-aware. For parents to guide children and help them to understand what sort of behaviours are and aren't acceptable.

So, it's important for parents and children to sit down and have an open discussion on what behaviour is acceptable and what isn't because each one of us has our own boundaries. Once we have defined these boundaries, it's important to use them as your early warning system.

The minute there's a certain behaviour that is stepping outside that boundary of comfort for you, you should be able to open up about it. Explain your dislike for it, while ensuring not only the person inflicting that behaviour on you knows about this but also anyone in an authority position knows about this, too.

With the amount of bullying awareness there is out there in the world, the minute you call another person a bully or tell them that their behaviour reflects that of a bully, it halts them. No one wants to be a bully.

How do we teach children to be strong when they are bullied and how do we get them to open up to the parent?

Parents need to set an example for their children of what acceptable and unacceptable behaviour is while also setting the example of what to do when one is subjected to unacceptable behaviour. Children do as parents do, not as they say. So, this learning starts at home.

It's equally important to create an environment in which children feel comfortable to be vulnerable. One of the reasons I've included letter samples in this book for teenagers is that if they cannot communicate with their parents, they can at least write a letter to explain how they feel.

Why do school hold assemblies on bullying and yet, when teachers see bullying first-hand, they do nothing to step up? It's usually the other students who step up.

It's one thing to preach, but it's another to put that into practice. Personally, I think there needs to be a system for teachers as well as students for bullying. Teachers need guidelines to differentiate between kids goofing around with each other vs. kids bullying other kids. Perhaps teachers expect the students to come up to them and actively seek help from them while students fear retaliation from bullies if they tell on them.

Possibly, there is a break in communication between teachers and students. That break in communication is something that needs to be bridged, and the only way we can do this is through training for both teachers and students.

Students need a step-by-step action plan that they can take when they are being bullied, whilst teachers need a step-by-step action plan for when they notice bullying. These action plans should be included as formal guides handed out at the beginning of a new school year. These guides should be reviewed and discussed in each class every month as a way of reinforcing the learning while also identifying loopholes.

What is the line between playing around and bullying? Sometimes it just starts out as playing around and then the next thing that kid is being accused of being a bully?

As I mentioned earlier, we all have our own personal boundaries between playing and bullying. Communication is the key - ensure those you spend the most time with are aware of your boundaries. So, if you're playing around and it escalates to something that you're not comfortable with, you have to voice your discomfort to the other kids.

Ensure they know that it's borderline bullying for you. The minute you say that the other person will back off. It is so important to know your own personal boundaries right at the beginning when things just start to get a little out of hand and uncomfortable. That is when you voice it, you don't wait for it to escalate.

What do you do if you're too scared to tell a parent or a teacher about the bullying because you're afraid it will escalate?

While I understand the fear associated with calling out a bully, it is important to note that "nothing changes if nothing changes" (Courtney C Stevens).

Tell a parent or teacher about the bullying, but at the same time, state your fears of retaliation. If those in charge know exactly what you're afraid of, they can keep an eye on you. If they don't know, they won't be able to keep tabs on you to ensure things haven't escalated.

The best way to overcome this fear is by writing it down. This helps to get it out of your heart and your mind and on paper. Stating your fears this way releases the power the fear has over you.

While it is perfectly okay to expect those in charge to come up with solutions, feel free to suggest your own. Things like separating you from your bully by placing you in separate groups. Perhaps they can ensure you are never alone with this person. Let them know that you're depending on them to help you out.

What if no one believes you?

There are two things you should in this case. First, gather evidence - whether that's voice recordings made discreetly on your phone or witnesses who are willing to attest to what you are battling. Secondly, keep asking for help and have the evidence handy to back your story up. Don't stop asking for help, support and guidance until you are satisfied with the action taken. Don't give up - the only person you'd be giving up on is yourself.

Schools have a no fighting policy - if a kid hits you first, is it okay to hit back?

No, it's not okay.

What you can do is holler on top of your voice and run like there's a fire burning close behind you. Shout and run to grab enough attention as possible. Fact is, if you hit back, you'll get suspended as well. But if you bring attention to what's happening, then you have witnesses who might take your side and it'll be the bully who will be punished for their actions, not you.

You don't want to get punished for it as well. Yes, I understand that you want to defend yourself. I'm not denying that. But the long-term consequences of defending yourself by hitting back is suspension from school which goes on your record which in turn may affect your admission to college. Do you really want that? Is it worth it? Don't cut off your nose to spite your face.

What do you do when someone accuses other kids of being bullies but she is the bully herself?

If she's the bully, there will be evidence of it. In such a situation, it so important to rally together against such a person and let them know that they are accusing others of being a bully - while they need to take a look at their own behaviour. There is strength in numbers.

More often than not, if the other kids are being called bullies by this one bully, it's because the other kids are trying to stand up against them and the bully is afraid of being called out.

Is it better to transfer and just start over?

I did it and I have no regrets at all. Once again, it all depends on your own personal situation. If you find that you've raised countless concerns about someone being a bully and appropriate action has been taken leading to things improving for you, then there's no need to transfer and start over.

However, if you find that the behaviour hasn't stopped, and it's persistent to the point where you have anxiety and you don't want to get up and go to school every day, then yes, transfer and start over. At the end of the day, if you don't stand up for yourself, nobody else is going to. You have to voice what you are uncomfortable with, just as I did. Know, trust and believe that there is nothing wrong with that, it takes immense courage to make such a decision. You do have that strength and courage to do what is right for you.

What about isolation?

Isolation is a very subtle form of bullying. I experienced this form of bullying as an adult from family members. How did I cope with it? I realised that there is no reason for me to feel crushed about being isolated by them because they showed me that they cannot accept and respect me the way I am. Why should I feel hurt about those who don't take me as I am? They did me a favour by isolating me, it was like the trash took itself out.

Put quite simply, those to whom you matter will always include and accept you, those to whom you don't matter will isolate you – why worry about the latter group? More likely than not, they don't even matter to you.

What about cyberbullying?

Screenshots. This is how you collect evidence against your bully, you have physical proof which they cannot negate. Collect this evidence and share it with a person who has the authority to take action against your bully.

Remember, if the bullying involves physical or sexual threats, it is a criminal offence and needs to be reported to the police as well.

Do they find it funny? Or does it just make them feel better? What does it do for them? Do they understand the repercussion it causes; teens have committed suicide over bullying? Have they ever been bullied? Do their parents somehow encourage it?

It's not so much that they find it funny, it's that it makes them feel better. Remember, happy people don't go around hurting other people.

I don't think they fully understand the repercussions of their behaviour, if they knew and understood that teens commit suicide over bullying, they would probably rethink their actions. They do it in a futile attempt to subdue the hurt that they feel within themselves. What they don't understand is that they cannot make themselves look better by making someone else look or feel bad.

Have they ever been bullied? Probably. And this is their response to it. They're just doing what was done to them. They're just practicing what they have learnt from behaviour towards them.

I don't think parents encourage it, but they sure as hell don't discourage it either. Sometimes, parents are responsible for creating a bully. Some parents feel that negative or reverse psychology can bring about a positive response in their child, but it doesn't. For example, some parents might call their child "dumb" or "stupid" in hopes to "motivate" them to "better" themselves whether at academics or sports. They assume that is going to make their child somehow smarter or work harder. It doesn't, those words hurt children and by being hurt, they just want to lash out, they want to make others feel how they feel. Bullies cannot rise to the level of their victims, so they try to bring their victims down to their level.

I cannot remember where I read this, but I wonder if it is something we could use on bullies. I don't know how far it is true but, apparently this is something that is practiced in some villages in Africa (I don't know which country in Africa).

When someone in that village has done something wrong, sometimes even a criminal offence, villagers make that person stand in the middle of a circle, surrounded by everyone who lives in that village. Going around in the circle, each person says a positive thing about the offender standing in the middle, whether it's a kind deed this person has done or an act of kindness they have shown.

Eventually, by the time everyone standing in the circle has said something nice about the offender, they're in tears. They have forgotten what a good person they were because of battling something within themselves. What if we did that with bullies? What if we put them in the middle of a circle and said something nice about them?

I know it is not the first thing that will come to mind when someone has hurt you. All you want to do is make them stop, you want to make them feel how you have felt.

I would like to add that forgiveness does not mean absolution for your bully. You're not absolving them of what they did, but you're letting go of the hurt, anger and bitterness you feel. Doing so will give you a quantum leap towards better days. Remember, you cannot create anything positive out of negative feelings.

How do you move on?

Before I even get into this topic, I think it is important to explain where I am today and how far I have come.

As you know, I went on to another boarding school. Though I had only two friends, it was better than none, and there was no bullying whatsoever in the new school. I graduated high school and went on to complete both an undergraduate degree and a postgraduate degree at university. During my university years, I was also crowned second runner up, amongst thousands, in the intervarsity queen competition and I was also elected a member to two committees within the Student Representative Council.

I was known and loved in university for not only being true to who I was but for being proud of it. After university, I completed my CPA (Certified Public Accountant) designation both in the UK and in Canada.

Many years later, I started strength training at home as part of my physical and mental wellbeing. My fitness story was featured on quite a few platforms with audiences in the hundreds of thousands. I went on to train and inspire close to 1,500 women from across the globe to take on a healthier lifestyle and to believe in themselves. Until recently, I had close to 3,000 followers on social media.

I say until recently because I walked from all of it to write this book. While it was great inspiring others in the fitness realm, I still felt empty inside. Despite having learnt and grown so much, there was still a yearning within me to do something, no matter how small, to make a difference.

It was mid-2018, around May when I wrote a short story of the bullying I faced in boarding school. This story was published across five hundred websites including local websites and international news sites such as Fox, ABC and NBC.

A few days after my story was published, a friend reached out to me. She had attended the same boarding school mentioned in this book and had also faced bullying. However, what she said to me, saddened me. She told me that moving on was hard for her. She still struggled with self-confidence and had self-esteem issues more than thirty years later. "How do you move on?" she asked.

And it's this question which I am hoping to answer for her and for all of you. How does one actually move on? How do you forget the pain and agony of the emotional battering you faced? Do you ever really forget?

Let's talk about the healing process. The first and foremost action anyone should take is doing whatever is necessary to put an end to the bullying. If this isn't possible then remove yourself from the situation in which you are being bullied. In my case, I spoke to whoever would listen - teachers, senior students, the principal, counsellors, literally anyone who would spare a minute to listen to me. I know that I did everything within my power to put an end to the bullying. When nothing was done to stop it, I removed myself from the situation. For the longest time, I saw myself as a failure - only the tough ones, including my brother, survived in that boarding school. I wasn't one of the tough ones, or so I thought.

It took many years to flip that mindset around, to come to the realisation that it takes a truly brave person to stand up to any injustice rather than to suffer in silence, just to fit in and just to be accepted.

I always chose to walk in the direction that I felt was right for me. Once you walk away from the bullying, the starting point is understanding that bullies are nothing but hurt people.

The point of understanding this very basic concept is this — there's nothing wrong with the victim at all, in fact, more often than not, there is everything "right" with the victim. The problem comes in because the bully cannot understand this and doesn't like that, hence they try to break their victims down, they try to dull their victim's shine.

As a victim of bullying myself, I constantly felt that there was something "wrong" with me and that is why I was targeted. This led to feelings of low self-esteem, feelings of being not "good enough" and an overall lack of confidence. Once I realised that there was something wrong with the bully and nothing wrong with me, that was when I could focus on the fact that what others say about me doesn't become my reality.

The second step is forgiving yourself. Don't beat yourself up about being a victim of bullying. No, you couldn't have been strong enough, tough enough, brave enough to do whatever you feel could've been done to prevent or even stop the bully. You were being true to yourself and being true to yourself means you don't stoop down to the level of your bully. In my case, I did what I was capable of, what my parents taught me to do - be respectful, don't fight. These values still hold true for me today.

Ensure you don't change your behaviour and your personality in response to your bully's words. Sometimes victims do this as they feel it will stop the bully from taunting them further while the bully's words shatter the victim's self-confidence and self-esteem. Changing who you are won't stop your bully.

Through the process of forgiving yourself, engage in confidence-building activities. This can be anything that gives you joy - I tried everything under the sun: hockey, swimming, volleyball, drawing, writing, singing, badminton. You name it, I did it. I finally found happiness in one sport – badminton. I went on to be ranked 2nd amongst all players at university level.

These are some valuable lessons I learnt which I wish to share:

- Be different, don't change just so that people will like you.
- Stay true to who you are, your strength lies in that.
- If you come across someone who is different, dare to befriend them. I can guarantee that you will learn so much from them.
- It doesn't matter what others think of you, what matters is what you think of yourself. What others say about you doesn't become your reality, it doesn't define who you are, unless if you let it.
- There's a very specific reason you're different. I encourage you to embrace it because being different will make a difference in this world.
- Asking for help doesn't make you a weak person. It takes an immensely strong person to seek help, to admit that they need help.

- You're not weak if you cry. This is especially true for boys.

Finally, when you're in the recovery process, it's so important to surround yourself with people who build you up. Your environment is key to your healing process. Pay attention to the kind of people you surround yourself with. There will be those who refuse to get involved, who refuse to validate how you feel - avoid these people. There will be a small handful who will encourage you, support you and guide you through your healing process – actively seek these people out, learn from them, give back to them, build yourself up while building others up. Be the change you wish to see. Even if there are very few of you, it starts with planting that seed of hope. Be that seed, be different, celebrate being different because this is the difference our world needs right now.

I chose to be different; I always voiced my thoughts against any form of injustice - in school, in university, in the workplace and in family. I always trusted my intuition and I always did what I felt was right and not what others thought I should do, not what society expected me to do. I am and always will be a rebel.

Today I am grateful for the person I have become because I fought hard to become her.

CLOSING THOUGHTS

- Persistence and consistency in seeking help when dealing with a bully will get you the results that you want. Keep applying the techniques used in this book, you will see results. As I said in the beginning, anything is only as good as the effort you put towards it.

- Every time you reach out to anyone in a position to help you, ensure you share with them a list of action you have taken, when you took and the results of that said action.

- Doing the above will show the person in authority that you are doing something to help yourself, to solve this on your own which in turn will encourage them to meet you halfway. People are more inclined to help those who help themselves.

- If ever anyone tells you to hurt yourself in any way, report it – to teachers, to your parents, to the parents of the teen who said it to you. Bring as much attention to this as possible. Please don't ignore this. This is very serious.

- Expanding on the above, I was told to "just die", I made the mistake of not telling anyone of this but somehow, I had my senses about myself not to take action on these words. All these years later, this person apologised to me, they were being teased by their friends every time I showed up for support. It doesn't justify what they said, nor does it absolve them of their deed, but it does give me some comfort knowing they didn't mean what they said.

- Remember – when someone tells you to hurt yourself, they don't mean it, it comes from the desperation of "trying to get to you". Let them be desperate, you don't fall for it.
- Don't give up, keep seeking help until you are satisfied with the action taken.

There is no justification or validation for consistent, insensitive behaviour towards another individual. You cannot expect others to believe in you if you don't believe in yourself. No more waiting, wishing, hoping and dreaming. Start here, start now - start living the happiest days of your life. It begins today, it starts now. Stop waiting for better days and start creating them instead.

"Believe you can, and you are halfway there."

~ Theodore Roosevelt. ~

RESOURCES

Need a quick fix to boost your mood, give you courage and strength through your battle or perhaps you wish to encourage a friend through their battle? Download "A Story of Hope":

- http://learnmoreabout.info/ASTORYOFHOPE

KEEP IN TOUCH

I hope you have enjoyed learning from this book, my best wishes are with you for every success. I would absolutely love to hear how this book has helped you. Feel free to share your success stories with me. You can connect with me through my Facebook page www.facebook.com/kalyanispeaks and follow my page to learn of upcoming workshops and events where I will be speaking.

Celebrating your success,

Kalyani Pardeshi

Made in the USA
Las Vegas, NV
08 December 2021

36571351R00095